D1219771

FOREIGN
POLICY
OF
POLAND
1919–39

FOREIGN
POLICY
OF
POLAND
1919–39

*From the Rebirth of the
Polish Republic to World War II*

ROMAN DEBICKI

With a Foreword by
Oscar Halecki

FREDERICK A. PRAEGER
Publisher • New York

DK 440
.D45

BOOKS THAT MATTER

Published in the United States of America in 1962 by
Frederick A. Praeger, Inc., Publisher
64 University Place, New York 3, N.Y.

© 1962 by Frederick A. Praeger, Inc.

All rights reserved

Library of Congress Catalog Card Number: 62–13732

Manufactured in the United States of America

PENNSYLVANIA MILITARY COLLEGE
CHESTER, PENNSYLVANIA
LIBRARY
53100

DISCARDED
WIDENER UNIVERSITY

*To the colleagues and friends
with whom I shared in the
effort to build up the foreign
service of the Polish Republic
and to secure for reborn Poland
her rightful place within the
family of nations.*

53100

Contents

Foreword

IT IS HARDLY surprising that until now there did not exist in any language a history of Poland's foreign policy during the twenty years of independence between the two World Wars. The international relations of the resurrected Republic were indeed so involved and so closely connected with all problems of general European, if not world, politics that their full presentation could not but appear an unusually difficult task. Nor is it surprising that in so many general works, the foreign affairs of Poland have been only too frequently misrepresented in a spirit not of sympathetic understanding but of greatly exaggerated, even unfair, criticism. This can be explained, to a large extent, by the regrettable, though understandable, fact that those responsible for Poland's relations with other countries proved unable—and sometimes, perhaps, unwilling—to make sufficiently clear to the outside world the real motives behind their actions and reactions in situations that never ceased to be dangerous or delicate.

This fact is pointed out, as are many others that have not received adequate attention before, in the present study of Poland's foreign policy by Professor Roman Debicki. Aware of all the difficulties such a pioneer work entails, he has wisely limited it to a preliminary survey. As such, it will certainly be a challenge to further investigations. His well-organized and well-written work is eminently successful, for two main reasons:

First, though obviously no attempt to exhaust the tremendous amount of material, his account is based on scholarly research in primary sources. These include not only the most recently published official documents and private memoirs but also previously unpublished information taken from, among other sources, the National Archives in Washington, D.C., and, particularly, from still-unpublished papers of Polish diplomats.

Second, Professor Debicki, before accepting his present position as Professor of Government at Georgetown University, was himself a Polish diplomat, occupying high posts in the Warsaw Foreign Office and serving as Minister Plenipotentiary in various capitals, both before the war and during its course. Especially in the 1930's, he had access to otherwise unavailable sources of information and frequent occasion to participate in important negotiations, so that the second part of his book is particularly original. So far as the origin and background of the war is concerned, the book is truly exciting reading, because of the author's well-balanced and objective approach. Professor Debicki's wartime experience contributed to a better understanding of the preceding events through his well-developed sense of the continuity of the historical process.

For a professional historian primarily interested in the earlier phases of Poland's history—in the long centuries of Poland's independence before the partitions—it will be interesting to note the factors of continuity and the recurrence of similar, though never quite identical, situations in the diplomatic history of a country that almost without interruption was threatened by Germany in the West and Russia in the East. There is, on the other hand, no continuity but, rather, a striking contrast between the foreign policy of former free Poland and what is called the foreign policy of today's Communist-controlled Poland. The former, in spite of the tense relations and repeated conflicts with her immediate Western neighbor, never turned against the Western world to which she belonged and which she served as a first line of defense. Communist Poland is forced by Moscow to serve as an outpost of an Eastern bloc, contrary to the real sympathies and desires of the Polish people.

Nothing could be of more help in understanding that contrast and the whole anomaly of Poland's present position in international affairs than the study of the leading principles of her foreign policy before the catastrophe of 1939. And this gives Professor Debicki's book its striking timeliness.

—OSCAR HALECKI

Preface

THIS BOOK has not been conceived as an exhaustive study of Poland's foreign policy between the two World Wars. My purpose is to provide the reader with a concise account of the diplomatic activity of successive Polish governments during that period, as observed by a close witness, and to present the general trends of Polish foreign policy against a background of the domestic and international circumstances that motivated them.

It is my earnest hope that this work will stimulate further studies that will, in turn, lead to better understanding and interpretation of Poland's foreign policy, rectifying opinions and judgments not always fair to that country.

My gratitude goes to the eminent historian Professor Oscar Halecki for reading and commenting on my manuscript, to its great benefit.

I am greatly indebted to Georgetown University and its Alumni Association, whose Annual Giving Fund supported the completion of this publication.

—R. D.

FOREIGN
POLICY
OF
POLAND
1919–39

I

The Rebirth of the State

THE STUDY OF Poland's foreign policy between the two World Wars requires a brief survey of the Polish people's endeavors, tendencies, and aims before the rebirth of their sovereign state. During the roughly 150 years when the territory of Poland was partitioned by Russia, Prussia, and Austria, the reunification of Polish lands into an independent state never ceased to be the ultimate aspiration of every Pole. Even when the last insurrection of the Polish people was crushed in 1864 and the Polish problem disappeared as an international issue, the spirit of the nation was not broken. But because of the losses suffered in life and property during the numerous armed uprisings of the nineteenth century, the Poles now turned to constructive effort—the slogan was "organic work"—in which all social classes participated. Breaking with the tradition of armed resistance, the Polish people concentrated on practical work in the social, economic, and educational fields. This period, lasting half a century, was marked by a considerable development of the social and cultural life of the nation.

Although being subordinated to the alien interests and economic systems of three partitioning powers was inimical to the normal growth and development of a modern nation, economic and cultural progress in all three sections of Poland was, by the end of the nineteenth century, almost equal to Austria's and certainly superior to Russia's. With the rising standard of living and the growth of social consciousness, the interest in political problems and the activity of political groups increased. In spite of reprisals by ruling authorities, who were anxious to suppress Polish national activities —especially in Russian and Prussian Poland—several political parties were created under the leadership of men who were later called on to play important roles in a reborn Poland.

At the outbreak of World War I, these were the most important

3

parties: (1) The National Democratic Party, created in 1897 under the leadership of Roman Dmowski, with a program based on nationalist aspirations combined with democratic ideals; particularly efficient and powerful in the Russian and German parts of Poland. (2) The Polish Socialist Party (PPS), created in 1892, which split into two parts after the abortive Russian revolution of 1905—one group composed of socialist elements with definite Polish patriotic tendencies, the other with leanings toward Russian revolutionary groups. (3) The Populist Party, representing the interests of the large peasant class and based on advanced rural programs; one of its leaders was Wincenty Witos, member of the Austrian Parliament and Prime Minister in several governments of reborn Poland. There were other political organizations of minor importance, with varying activities and ramifications in all three sections of partitioned Poland.

Few peoples found themselves in a more complicated and difficult situation than the Poles in 1914. Drafted against their will into the armies of their oppressors, they still showed a determination to avail themselves of every opportunity to throw off the foreign bondage. It was clear that the armed conflict between Poland's two main enemies—Germany and Russia—offered a unique opportunity for her liberation.

As to the methods of attaining the independence and reunification of Polish territories, two main currents of opinion appeared at the very beginning of the war: The National Democratic Party was in favor of complete solidarity with the Entente powers, including collaboration with Russia for the defeat of Germany, whom they considered Poland's chief enemy; Galicia became the focus of those elements that expected the victory of the Central powers, based their liberation program on a federation with Austria-Hungary, and supported the Polish Legions created by Józef Piłsudski to fight against Russia. Piłsudski's ultimate aim, however, was the total liberation and independence of Poland, without any link with the partitioning powers. At the beginning of World War I, his program was looked upon by many as but a romantic dream, and yet the unpredictable outcome of the war brought about its full realization.

The disappearance of Poland from the map of Europe in the eighteenth century was a result of both the concurrent decision of the partitioning powers and their overwhelming strength. As if in fulfillment of historical justice, the long struggle of the Poles to recover their independence came to an end when the victory of the Entente in World War I brought about the defeat of Germany and the breaking up of the Austro-Hungarian Empire. These events, and the revolutionary chaos prevailing in Russia from 1917 onward, enabled the Poles to break away from their oppressors at the end of 1918. They possessed sufficient vitality and determination for the reconstruction of their state. What they needed was diplomatic recognition and admission to the society of nations.

Since neither the national consciousness of the Poles nor their resolve to unite and resume their sovereign existence as a nation-state had weakened, they were prepared beforehand for the task that faced them after the war. Using various tactics adapted to the circumstances, they had taken an active part in the pursuit of the war politically and, in a limited way, militarily. Polish leaders had established early contacts with leading members of the Entente governments. Their efforts had been directed toward achieving recognition of Poland as a full-fledged Allied nation in the eventual peace negotiations.

From October, 1917, onward, Poland had a recognized representation in the camp of the Entente—the Polish National Committee in Paris. In Poland itself there existed a Regency Council, established by the Central powers, with a government appointed by the Regents.

The origin of the Paris Committee goes back as far as 1914, when a Polish Relief Committee was formed at Vevey, Switzerland, by outstanding Polish patriots like Ignace Jan Paderewski, Henryk Sienkiewicz, Antoni Osuchowski, and others. This Committee soon became a center of Polish activities in the West, not only in the humanitarian field but also in the political field. In August, 1916, at a meeting in Lausanne, the decision was taken to create a Polish National Committee. Paris was chosen as the seat of the Committee, of which Roman Dmowski became Chairman and Maurice Zamoyski Vice-Chairman. The members were Joseph

Wielowieyski, Marian Seyda, Dr. F. Fronczak (representative of the American Poles), Erazm Piltz (delegate to the French Government), Ladislas Sobanski (delegate in London), and Konstanty Skirmunt (delegate in Rome). Paderewski, also a member of the board, was appointed the Committee's delegate to Washington.

Having notified the Allied governments of its formation and outlined its aims, the Committee received recognition as an official Polish organization from France, Great Britain, Italy, and the United States.[1] After the Treaty of Brest, in March, 1918, the Committee was strengthened in its diplomatic position and found new opportunities for action. The Polish problem could now be examined and dealt with by France, England, and Italy without the restrictions inherent in Russian tendencies. The Allied governments openly supported Polish independence, which President Wilson had advocated a year before. The United States had taken the lead in the Polish question in 1918. Point Thirteen of President Wilson's message to Congress on January 8, 1918, was of enormous importance to Poland as a forerunner to his leadership in the subsequent peace negotiations.[2] But this did not yet mean the official commitment of the Allied powers, a commitment the Poles were extremely anxious to secure. This came on June 3, 1918, in the declaration by the heads of the French, British, and Italian governments assembled at Versailles; they agreed that "the creation of a united and independent Poland with free access to the sea constitutes one of the conditions of a solid and just peace, and the rule of right in Europe."[3]

This declaration was the result of a just appreciation by the Allied powers of the part that Poland had to play under the conditions prevailing in Central and Eastern Europe after Russia's defection. The persistent and efficacious efforts of the Polish National Committee in Paris had been instrumental in shaping the opinion and the decisions of the Western statesmen with regard to Poland. The Committee's members were able to gain access to political leaders of the Entente, to hold their attention, and to win their confidence. They did not limit their activities to the problems of Poland alone, but endeavored to influence all the decisions concerning Central and Eastern European territorial questions, expressing the needs and aims of oppressed or artificially divided nationalities.[4] More and more, the Committee was able to step forth as the authorized spokesman for the Polish nation. Its delegates in Washington, Rome, and London, well prepared for their tasks, reached a high political standing and were treated almost as Poland's accredited envoys. It was equally successful in assuming the protection of Poles in the Entente countries. Through agreements arrived at with the respective governments, additional offices closely resembling consulates were created by the Committee in London, New York, Paris, and Rome for the purpose of providing Poles with passports and other documents and giving them some degree of protection.

When the Polish Army in France expanded and the necessity arose of providing it with a political head, the National Committee's prestige made possible the conclusion of official agreements with the French Government concerning the Committee's authority over military matters.[5] About 20,000 Americans of Polish descent volunteered to join the Polish troops in France. The army thus formed was officially recognized by all the Entente powers as "autonomous, allied, and co-belligerent." This army and the net of diplomatic representations—politically subordinate to the National Committee—were valuable Polish assets toward the end of World War I and on the eve of the Peace Conference of Paris. When the hard work of the political reconstruction of Europe began, Poland was already entitled to take part in the deliberations of the victorious nations.

If the growth of the National Committee to the status of an unofficial department of foreign affairs turned out to be of special value for Poland when the defeat of the Central powers became inevitable, the existence of the German-sponsored Regency Council in Warsaw proved to be of no less importance at this crucial moment. It provided the country with a nucleus of governmental organization able to assume control at the very moment of Germany's collapse. It could proceed immediately to build a regular state administration and to take measures for the defense and liberation of Poland's territory.

The establishment of the Regency Council had been a consequence of the Austro-German proclamation of a Polish Kingdom, known as the Two Emperors' Manifesto,[6] a step prompted by the German Government primarily for military reasons. The mounting losses of the Central powers' armies required immediate measures for obtaining replacements, and the only apparent solution was to draw on Polish manpower in the former Russian provinces where mobilization had been only partially effected. By creating a puppet Polish state, they expected to be able to raise an army of several hundred thousand men within that territory. But the Polish people viewed the creation of a German-sponsored Polish state with indifference and suspicion. The truth about German intentions was clearly shown by an appeal to the Poles, published only four days after the Manifesto, to volunteer for a "Polish" army. As a consequence, fewer than 2,000 men applied for enlistment.[7] The Germans, quick to recognize their failure, attempted to redress the situation by making concessions to the Poles. To satisfy the claim that only a Polish government could appeal for voluntary enrollment in the Polish Army, a provisional Council of State was appointed on January 14, 1917. A few days later, the Council sent an enthusiastic telegram of thanks to President Wilson for his message of January 22. Pilsudski had accepted the chairmanship of the Council's military commission, which was expected to act as a sort of defense ministry. The German authorities did not realize that the failure of their recruiting program was a result of events in Russia. Once the fight against Russia was over, the Poles did not intend to back the Central powers with arms. It appeared, moreover, that all military matters were being handled by German officers. When the question of an oath of allegiance to be imposed on the Polish volunteers was brought up, Pilsudski resigned in protest. As a consequence, he was arrested on July 22 and imprisoned in the fortress of Magdeburg, in Germany, together with his Chief of Staff, Colonel Sosnkowski.

Soon afterward, the Council of State resigned. In October, 1917, the Germans, aware of the resentment of the Polish people, tried to neutralize the effect of the Entente powers' recognition of the National Polish Committee in Paris by appointing a Regency

Council. It was composed of three Polish notables—Alexander Cardinal Kakowski, Archbishop of Warsaw; Prince Z. Lubomirski; and Count J. Ostrowski. The Regents subsequently appointed a Polish government, headed by Jan Kucharzewski, a distinguished historian. From the start, the Regency Council had lacked the support of important political groups, but the Regents were anxious for Poland to appear on the international scene as an organized state, and this was an opportune time to create a national administration. In spite of their precarious position, they succeeded in extending their authority and in obtaining important rights from the occupation governments. Step by step, they gained control over educational, judicial, social, and even commercial and financial affairs. After the end of hostilities between Russia and the Central powers, the Germans no longer needed to please the Poles by making concessions to the Regency Council, and there was no hope for a further extension of the Council's authority. The Regents considered resigning, but decided to remain in office to maintain the degree of sovereignty and independence that they had acquired for Poland.

When Pilsudski, released by the Germans from the fortress of Magdeburg, arrived in Warsaw on November 10, 1918, the Regency Council immediately appointed him Commander in Chief of the army. Pilsudski's popularity had grown considerably during his imprisonment. His prestige as creator and commander of the Polish Legions, his links with the strong and popular Polish Socialist Party, and his outstanding personality singled him out for the role of leader. Three days after his return to Poland, the Regency Council resigned, investing him with the supreme civil authority. Pilsudski became Chief of State.

The final victory of the Entente and the complete collapse of the Central powers brought an end to German rule in Poland. Within a few days, the heart of the Polish lands was free. But a long struggle for the western and eastern borders was just beginning on the battlefields and around the conference tables. Despite their desire to set about rebuilding their ruined country in peace, the Polish people first had to bring their national territories together through protracted and difficult negotiations as well as armed struggle. Thus, in the initial period of her national reconstruction, Poland's foreign and military policies were inextricably mingled. Because Pilsudski was both Chief of State and chief of the army, Polish foreign policy responded to the momentary necessities of the military situation. On the other hand, strategic moves depended on political considerations, and military decisions took into account the current realities and trends in the international field.

Until the surrender of the Central powers and the Armistice of November 11, 1918, it was understandable that the National Committee in Paris should be the principal spokesman for Polish interests. The whole of Poland was occupied by Germany and Austria, and the government in Warsaw was a pawn of the Germans. The Committee, however, did not represent all political and social currents in Poland. It enjoyed the unreserved support of the two most important rightist parties, but it was strongly opposed by the leftist camp, led by the Polish Socialist Party. After the surrender to Pilsudski of the short-lived radical government in Lublin, and after the appointment of a more moderate socialist cabinet with Moraczewski at its head, it became clear that the source of political thought and activity must be shifted from abroad to Poland itself. Unity of action in foreign policy was an urgent necessity. For the approaching Peace Conference, where decisions about Poland's frontiers would be made, a comprehensive program of the nation's territorial aspirations had to be elaborated, put into execution, and defended.

In order to investigate the situation in Poland and to establish contact with other political groups and parties, the Polish National Committee sent to Warsaw one of its members, a former socialist, Stanislaw Grabski, who knew Pilsudski personally. Simultaneously, a delegation was dispatched by Pilsudski to Paris. But the role of peacemaker between the two camps was reserved for Paderewski.

Having returned to Paris from the United States in mid-December, 1918, Paderewski proceeded immediately to Poland in order to throw his authority and high repute into the reconciling of party differences and formation of a unified government. Pilsudski entered at once into negotiations with Paderewski and, on January 16, 1919, appointed him Prime Minister and Minister of Foreign Affairs.

To perform the regular duties of a foreign minister and to organize the urgently needed Polish representations abroad, Paderewski had to extend considerably the Ministry of Foreign Affairs inherited from the Regency Council. A nucleus of a foreign office had existed in Warsaw since January, 1918, under the name of the Department of State, but the German authorities had not permitted it to grow into a regular foreign ministry. On the contrary, the decree creating the Regency Council had categorically prohibited foreign representation by Polish authorities until the end of the state of occupation. But in the late summer and autumn of 1918, the deteriorating situation of the Central powers made it possible for the Regency Council to act more independently. On October 26, without consulting the occupation authorities, it appointed a Minister of Foreign Affairs. In November, 1918, a committee was established to select the best-trained and most acceptable candidates for the foreign service.[8] Besides a university degree, a good knowledge of at least two foreign languages was required. No party influences were considered in the choice of candidates. Several Poles from the Russian diplomatic service and others from the Austro-Hungarian consular service were gladly accepted and proved extremely valuable at the beginning of the organizational period of the Polish foreign service. But the number of politically trained and experienced persons available at that time was small. The personnel requirements of the Ministry could be satisfied only after the return to Poland of the people who had been active in the various Polish institutions abroad, as well as those who had completed their political or juridical studies in foreign countries during the war or had worked abroad for the Polish cause.

The Polish National Committee, provisionally left in charge of representation among the Western powers, became the delegation to the Peace Conference, with Dmowski and Paderewski acting as Poland's chief delegates. Dr. Dluski, Pilsudski's personal friend and political adherent, acted as a substitute for Paderewski, whose duties often kept him in Warsaw. The diplomatic missions representing the Committee in various countries were subordinated to the Warsaw Ministry of Foreign Affairs and gradually transformed into regular legations following recognition of the Polish state by the foreign powers.

The United States was first to recognize Poland and its government. Secretary of State Lansing sent a note to Paderewski to this effect on January 22, 1919.[9] Within a few weeks, America's example was followed by the majority of powers. Poland was now recognized as an independent state, but it was a state with undetermined frontiers.

The problems with which Poland was faced from the first day of her liberation were overwhelming and immediate. The most urgent was the evacuation of German occupation troops. Thanks to Pilsudski's personal effort and his knowledge of the soldier's psychology, this problem was resolved quickly and satisfactorily. The German Soldiers' Council agreed to the disarmament and orderly withdrawal of the troops, in return for Pilsudski's promise of protection and transportation facilities for the German soldiers returning home. Within a week, central Poland was free of foreign troops; and the stocks of armaments and munitions left by the Germans were a great help in the organization of a national army. But, to the east and north of the Polish territory, the Baltic countries, White Ruthenia, and the Ukraine were still occupied by powerful German armies,[10] and these troops began to move west in a disorderly manner as they heard news of the revolution in Germany. It was essential for Poland to secure their withdrawal as rapidly as possible by a route that would spare the Polish population new hardships and preserve the country from looting and the destruction of its meager resources by the demoralized German soldiers.

Despite their defeat on the Western Front, their surrender to the Entente, and the revolutionary movements inside Germany, the Germans endeavored to save as much as possible of their political influence in the east. As early as November 19, 1918, a "plenipotentiary" of the Berlin government, Count Harry Kessler, appeared in Warsaw.[11] The government of Moraczewski was taken by surprise and greatly embarrassed. It was dangerous at that stage to repudiate a mission, whose presence could be—as this one eventually became—advantageous in the negotiations concerning the withdrawal of the German Army in the east. On the other hand, the population resented intensely the presence of a representative of the enemy in Warsaw. Kessler's presence even provoked a divergence of opinion inside the Foreign Ministry that culminated in the resignation of the Undersecretary of State, Filipowicz.[12] Finally, on December 15, 1918, Count Kessler was asked to leave the country, thus causing an interruption of Polish-German relations. But in the meantime an agreement had been worked out for the withdrawal of the German Army through communication lines well to the north of Poland's center. In February, 1919, the evacuation was completed.

The second immediate problem was eastern Galicia, where an armed struggle between Ukrainians and Poles had begun in November, 1918. In Galicia, as in the rest of Austria-Hungary after the collapse of the monarchy, a local administration was established to take over the functions of the withdrawing Austrian officials. This was expected to be all the easier since Galicia had had an autonomous, predominantly Polish administration under Austrian rule, with Lwów serving as the capital. The problem of taking over the civil and military powers was solved in the western part of the province, but not in Lwów and in the eastern districts, with their mixed Polish and Ukrainian population.

The majority of the population of Lwów was Polish, while Ukrainians were in the majority in the rural districts of eastern Galicia. During the war, the Ukrainians had formed a political council, the Ukrainian National Rada, under the leadership of Eugene Petrushevytch. Like the Poles, who had formed the Legions as the nucleus of their future army, the Ukrainians had organized volunteer units, called Sitchovi Striltsi (Sitch Sharpshooters), to prepare for the moment when an independent state could be created out of territories divided between Russia and Austria-Hungary.

But Austria, even in the last days of her existence, still used her political method of divide and rule on Poles and Ukrainians, the two nationalities that had lived for centuries in eastern Galicia. Count Huyn, the Austrian Governor of Galicia, handed over the Lwów central offices to the Ukrainians without giving notice to the Poles. The Ukrainians then proclaimed the Republic of Western Ukraine. They could not, however, establish control over the city. The population of Lwów improvised an armed resistance, in which mostly young people took part, and defended the town and the suburbs until the arrival first of reinforcements from other parts of the country and finally of regular Polish troops. On November 21, Lwów was occupied by the Poles, and the Rada withdrew farther east to continue the fight.

But the struggle for Lwów became a source of bitterness between Poles and Ukrainians. It also became an obstacle to the solution of the southeastern border of Poland. In due course, this problem was dealt with by the Peace Conference. Several alternatives were put forward: division of the territory, a plebiscite, a twenty-five-year mandate for Poland. An Allied commission arranged an armistice, but fighting broke out again and again. Finally, the Supreme Council, fearing intervention by Bolshevik Russia, recognized "the pressing necessity to keep the Bolsheviks out," and authorized the Polish Government, on June 25, 1919, to establish its authority over the whole province.[13] After protracted discussions in the League of Nations, Polish sovereign rights over this territory were recognized on March 15, 1923, by the Conference of Ambassadors, with provision for an autonomous administration.

Revolutionary Russia had recognized Poland's independence in principle, but it was soon evident that the old Czarist imperialism had merely been transformed into a new one, with revolutionary slogans. A great part of Lithuania and White Ruthenia, as well as parts of Latvia and Estonia, were overrun by Red troops and organized in the well-known Communist pattern.[14] The town of Vilna—which even the Germans, in their proclamation when they occupied it in 1915, had called a "pearl of the Kingdom of Poland" —was taken on January 5, 1919, by the Bolsheviks, who then proceeded toward Grodno. Wherever the eastern boundaries of the reconstituted Polish state were eventually to be established (the victorious Entente powers were to delimit them as a last resort),[15] the steady advance of the Red Army became a serious menace to Poland. Massacres and savage cruelties were inflicted upon the inhabitants, especially the Polish groups. If the advance was not checked, it would result in the loss of eastern territories claimed by Poland and would threaten the very existence of the young Polish republic. The Bolsheviks' intention was to destroy the existing political order and undermine the social and economic structure of Europe. The only alternative for Poland was to organize such military forces as were available in those formative months and to oppose the further progress of the Red Army. At the beginning of 1919, a Russo-Polish *de facto* front came into being. Thus Poland became involved in an armed conflict that was to last for almost two years and culminate in what an unbiased observer has called the eighteenth decisive battle of the world.[16]

At the same time that these military and diplomatic efforts had to be undertaken in defense of her eastern territories, it was essential that Poland set forth her claims concerning her western frontiers. In Poznan and Pomerania, the Poles were in a most difficult position. Article 12 of the Armistice Agreement of November 11, 1918, provided only for the withdrawal of the German Army from the east to the frontiers of 1914; it did not even mention the Polish territories held by Prussia. This stipulation had been dictated by the apprehension existing in Entente circles, and even among some members of the National Committee, that Eastern European territories would become, after Germany's withdrawal, a field of chaos and of Bolshevik invasion. It is true that another article of the Armistice provided for access to Poland by Allied forces through the port of Danzig and the Vistula valley. But the Germans consistently opposed the application of this article, and it remained a dead letter, especially during specific discussions about the route to Poland to be taken by the Polish Army in France, the so-called Haller Army.[17]

To prevent protracted German rule in the entirely Polish provinces of Poznan and Pomerania, the well-organized local people collaborated with and infiltrated the revolutionary Soldiers' and Workers' Councils that were being set up. A Polish Supreme

Popular Council was formed, and its executive committee became the nucleus of a Polish administration. When Paderewski, on his way from Paris to Warsaw, arrived in Poznan (via Danzig) on December 26, 1918, great ovations went up in his honor, and public tribute was paid to the Entente powers. This provoked a strong reaction in the Germans, and a minor incident led certain German officials to begin firing into the crowd. This, in turn, set off a general uprising of the Poles. The German garrison was turned out of Poznan, and the insurrection extended over the whole province. Battles were fought for all the important centers, and the struggle was terminated only when Marshal Foch forced an armistice upon the Germans on February 16, 1919, establishing a demarcation line between the Poles and the Germans. Poznan and the conquered major part of the province remained under a local Polish administration, but until the signing of the Treaty of Versailles, Polish territories that had been held by Prussia could not legally be incorporated into Poland.

At another point on Poland's western borders, Teschen Silesia, an armed conflict flared up unexpectedly in January, 1919. In October, 1918, the two nationalities of this province, Poles and Czechs, had created their own local government, which took over power from the Austrian authorities. The Polish and the Czech National Councils (Rada Narodowa and Narodni Vybor, respectively) had concluded an agreement on November 5, 1918, concerning the delimitation of their respective territories, based on a fair evaluation of the numerical distribution of the two nationalities. When the Peace Conference convened, the Czechoslovak and Polish delegations presented their claims to Teschen. The Poles based their claim on ethnic considerations, while the Czechs advanced economic reasons and demanded parts of the province inhabited mostly by Poles.

The Czechs, conscious of the weakness of their arguments, did not wait for a decision from the Peace Conference but set about creating an accomplished fact. On January 23, 1919, superior Czechoslovak forces attacked the Polish garrisons by surprise and, a few days later, occupied Teschen and several important centers of the province. Poland appealed to the Supreme Council, and under its auspices an arrangement providing for a provisional partition of the territory was signed in Paris. Nevertheless, in violation of the agreement, the Czechs attacked along the whole delimitation line again a month later. This time, the Poles recovered the city of Teschen, and a new convention was signed. But the controversy was not yet settled. Several proposals for a plebiscite or an award by the King of Belgium were advanced and rejected by one party or the other.

An explanation for Prague's bold tactics can be found in the assurance given to Czechoslovakia by France. As early as June, 1918, Pichon, the French Minister of Foreign Affairs, had promised, in an official letter to Dr. Benes, to back the Czechs fully in their aspirations for independence within their historical frontiers. In the summer of 1920, at the Conference of Spa, Poland suffered a final defeat on the question of Teschen. Pressed by the adverse situation in her war with the Bolsheviks, she had to assume various difficult obligations in return for a promise of help from the great powers. Among those obligations was the acceptance of an award on Teschen. This award, pronounced by the Conference of Ambassadors on July 28, 1920, gave Czechoslovakia the major part of the disputed territory, even though it had a large Polish population.

Thus the settlement of the Teschen problem was one of the first examples of political success achieved by a forcible *fait accompli,* and it proved the disregard of the great powers for ethnic principles. Because of this inequitable solution, relations between Poland and Czechoslovakia became embroiled, to the detriment of both nations. Subsequent events proved the truth of the almost prophetic words of Paderewski, who, in accepting the sentence on Teschen in behalf of Poland, wrote to Millerand—at that time Chairman of the Supreme Council—that "the decision of the Conference of Ambassadors had dug an abyss between the two nations."[18]

The problem of Teschen illustrates the complexity of territorial questions concerning Poland. The spontaneous rebirth of the Polish state after the collapse of the Central powers owed much to the vitality of the Polish nation, but the demarcation of its territorial limits depended on the Peace Conference. In spite of their sympathy for the Polish cause, the main Allied powers were not always in agreement with Polish claims. Thus Poland had to engage in intense diplomatic activity and overcome many difficulties in order to obtain more or less satisfactory solutions.

The principal Allied powers whose resolutions were decisive for the Conference each held a different view and interpretation of the principle of self-determination. The application of this principle also presented great difficulties. The central, and to an even greater degree the eastern, regions of the European continent are characterized by a lack of natural frontiers separating the several national groups; moreover, there is such an intermingling of nationalities and so many ethnic islands that it is almost impossible to establish boundary lines on purely ethnic principles.

The determination of Poland's frontiers was especially difficult. A state had to be rebuilt from territories that had been part of three different empires for several generations. It was considered impossible to solve the problem by simply reconstituting Poland according to her prepartition frontiers of 1772. The ethnic composition within these boundaries had undergone changes; only small Polish minorities remained in the region of the Dnieper and the Dvina, which had been taken from Poland in the eighteenth century, and the local populace would now resent being united with her. On the other hand, in Prussian Silesia, which had been separated from Poland long before the partitions, a strong national consciousness stirred its compact Polish population, even though this feeling was a development of recent decades.

Polish leaders had an intimate knowledge of the conditions necessary for rebuilding a strong, independent Poland. They began very early to explain the problem of Poland to the leading Western political circles. In July, 1917, Dmowski wrote and distributed among the most important leaders of the Entente powers an extensive memorandum on the postwar organization of Central and Eastern Europe. This document contained a penetrating analysis of the principles on which that area should be reconstructed in conformity with historical facts and evolutionary trends. One chapter consisted of a thorough explanation of the territorial problems of Poland.

At the time of the Armistice of November, 1918, Dmowski was in the United States. Conscious of the great influence that America, and President Wilson personally, would exert at the approaching Peace Conference, he endeavored to make Poland's territorial needs and aims known in detail to leading Americans. Upon the request of President Wilson himself, Dmowski drew up for him a project for the territorial settlement of the new Polish republic.[19]

Dmowski's recommendations became the principal basis of the Polish delegation's efforts and activities during the Peace Conference. Dmowski himself, as a delegate, and Paderewski, as Prime Minister of Poland, presented the Polish point of view before the Supreme Council, composed of the representatives of the five principal powers, and in the different commissions of the Conference.

The first session of the Peace Conference took place on January 18, 1919. Four days later, the Supreme Council, in response to a suggestion by the Polish Government, appointed an Inter-Allied Commission to go to Poland immediately for the purpose of studying at first hand her problems and needs.[20] The first occasion to sum up Poland's case and to outline the boundaries that would correspond to principles of justice as well as the economic and political necessities of the renovated state was given to the Polish delegation on January 29, 1919. On the invitation of the Supreme Council, Dmowski discussed at length the conditions prevailing in Poland—her temporary problems and needs, and the ethnic, social, and economic aspects of her territorial aims.[21] As a result, a Commission on Polish Affairs was appointed, under the chairmanship of Jules Cambon, to undertake the task of preparing recommendations for the German-Polish frontier.

In March, the Commission reported to the Supreme Council that it unanimously recommended the outright assignment to Poland of Danzig, part of West Prussia, strips of East Prussia, almost the whole of Poznan, and practically all of Upper Silesia along a frontier line corresponding to the limits of the Polish population. The Commission's only doubt with regard to the Polish-German frontier concerned the region of Allenstein (Polish: Olsztyn), the southern strip of East Prussia, and it recommended that the wishes of the people be ascertained through a plebiscite. The population of Allenstein, although unquestionably of Polish stock, was Protestant and had been separated from the rest of Poland for centuries. Doubts existed, therefore, as to its willingness to be reunited with the Polish state.

The attitudes of the great powers' delegations toward the Commission's report and proposals demonstrated their profound differences over East and Central European problems.

The American delegation appeared not to favor plebiscites as a means of determining the people's will. Although they urged the establishment of frontiers that followed the lines of cleavage between nationalities and although they regarded President Wilson's principles as binding, the American delegates and experts relied on ethnic data, which they had methodically gathered, and sought immediate decisions rather than plebiscites (with their inherent risk of delays and difficulties). However, in the case of Allenstein, they supported the British delegation's suggestion of a plebiscite, because they felt that the Polish claims for outright annexation of this region were based mainly on political considerations that were not sufficiently substantiated.

In general, the British delegation seemed to favor plebiscites, especially in determining the Polish-German frontier. At the end of March, their attitude stiffened under the personal influence of David Lloyd George. In his memoirs, Lloyd George admits that he challenged some of the unanimous conclusions of the Commission on Polish Affairs and that this gave rise to a fundamental discussion. He admits also to having exercised pressure on the Conference to reject the Commission's recommendations.[22] Lloyd George argued that the Germans would refuse to sign the treaty if Poland was allotted Danzig and Upper Silesia outright. He was also apprehensive about the attitude of the British Parliament, particularly the Labour Party members. The traditional balance-of-power policy of Great Britain obviously inclined the British delegation toward policies that would tend to create neither a

Germany too weak nor a France too strong, and it was to be expected that a strong Poland would become a complement and a natural ally of France in Eastern Europe. In spite of his ignorance of East European problems (he admitted in the House of Commons that he had "never heard of Teschen"),[23] Lloyd George stubbornly fought against Wilson and Clemenceau at the Peace Conference, and at his insistence the original drafts prepared by the territorial commission were modified, step by step, to the disadvantage of Poland.

It is difficult to judge whether the attitude of the British Prime Minister was dictated mainly by personal prejudice and insufficient knowledge of international affairs or by political considerations.[24] But it is clear that his insistence provoked a series of difficulties inside the Supreme Council; and in the final decision of the Conference, important concessions were secured, to Germany's advantage, in the question of Upper Silesia and Danzig.

France gave the strongest support to Poland during the Conference. Her historic friendship with the Polish nation, as well as the German menace that threatened both countries alike, provided the main motives for her favorable attitude toward Poland in the Polish-German territorial questions. The French delegation supported almost all the solutions essential to satisfying Poland's needs. The only instance in which France definitely opposed Polish claims, based on a clear-cut ethnographical line, was Teschen.

It was an arduous task for the Polish delegation to defend the interests of Poland amid the contradictory tendencies of the great powers. The lengthy polemics and bargaining among the members of the Supreme Council, the vehement protests of the German delegation, and the insistence of the British Prime Minister on further concessions to Germany combined to produce decisions much less favorable to Poland than could have been expected at the beginning of the Peace Conference. When Paderewski and Dmowski were invited to sign the Treaty of Versailles (June 28, 1919), its stipulations concerning Poland were considerably different from those drafted by the Commission on Polish Affairs.

A plebiscite was to be held not only in Allenstein but also in

Marienwerder and Upper Silesia. Danzig was not awarded to Poland, but was to become a free city. Modifications of the frontier of West Prussia had narrowed the so-called Polish Corridor.

If the loss of Allenstein and Marienwerder was not of vital importance to Poland, the Supreme Council's decision for a plebiscite in Upper Silesia constituted a major victory for Germany. After the signing of the treaty, the Germans used every possible artifice to retain this valuable industrial province. An insurrection of the Polish masses was brutally stifled by German regular troops, but Upper Silesia remained in a state of unrest. The national antagonism was reinforced by social divergences. The peasants and workers were almost exclusively Polish, whereas the landowners and industrial executives were Germans. Two more uprisings broke out, and fighting was stopped only by the intervention of the Inter-Allied Commission. The plebiscite, however, was held without disturbance on March 20, 1921.

The events in Upper Silesia provoked serious tension between France and Great Britain. Finally, the question was submitted to the Council of the League of Nations. Its recommendation, based on the report of a committee of four, was confirmed by the Conference of Ambassadors and subsequently accepted by Berlin and Warsaw. It provided for the division of Upper Silesia. Germany was allotted about 75 per cent of the area, with 57 per cent of the population, and Poland acquired the remainder, which contained the bulk of the industrial works, mines, and factories. Both countries agreed to the Geneva Convention of May 15, 1922, intended to preserve the economic stability of Upper Silesia during a transitional period of fifteen years. It contained, among other stipulations, detailed provisions for the protection of minority rights. An Arbitration Tribunal and a Mixed Commission were created to supervise the observance of the Convention.

Poland was already under the international control of the League of Nations in matters concerning minorities within its borders, having signed at Versailles on June 28, 1919, a special treaty with the principal Allied and Associated Powers. But no such general obligation had been imposed on Germany. Consequently, Poland became the target of constant German demands and accusations at the League of Nations, whereas the Polish minority in Germany—with the exception of the Poles in the German part of Upper Silesia—had no such international protection.

On the question of Danzig, the experts in charge of preliminary studies were unanimously of the opinion that the only way to assure the independence of Poland and the prosperity of Danzig was to restore this harbor city to Poland. It was clear to them that for Poland, which occupied the whole basin of the Vistula and centered on that single river, the laws of geography dictated the possession of its estuary. They realized also that Danzig under German rule had been restricted in its development and had sunk to a second-rate provincial town.[25]

The conclusion of the experts, pointing to the necessity of uniting Danzig with the reconstructed Polish state for historic, geographic, and economic reasons, appeared in the report of the Commission on Polish Affairs submitted to the Supreme Council on March 12, 1919. This was the only instance in which the Commission proposed a deviation from an ethnographic frontier line. Its members had agreed that it was more important to secure free access to the sea for a nation of more than 20 million people than to maintain a land connection between Germany and the 2 million East Prussians, whose trade was conducted mostly by sea. But the recommendation was vehemently opposed by the British Prime Minister, Lloyd George. Through his exertions, the Supreme Council agreed to make Danzig a free city, politically autonomous and economically united with Poland. The Free City was to be under protection of the League of Nations, whose High Commissioner was to participate in the drafting of a constitution by the local authorities. He would reside in Danzig and mediate between the Free City and Poland. A convention between Danzig and Poland would determine their reciprocal relations. Poland would have unhampered use of the port, and Danzig was to be included in the Polish customs system. The Polish Government would assume the foreign representation of the Free City.

The Danzig solution can be considered the most ill-fated decision taken by the Supreme Council. Satisfactory to none of the parties concerned, it later proved to be a source of endless complication and finally served as a pretext for the outbreak of World War II.

In regard to the eastern boundaries of Poland, the tendency of the Allied powers was to delay settlement, not only because of their differences of opinion but also because of the uncertainty of developments in Russia. This problem, of utmost importance in maintaining peace in Eastern Europe, was dealt with in Section 3 of Article 87 of the Treaty of Versailles. It reserved the right of the principal Allied and Associated Powers to decide the eastern frontiers of Poland at a later, undetermined date. In that way, the Allies stressed their belief that they had to determine all postwar problems, whatever they were and wherever they arose. But, at the same time, they left the solution of this difficult problem to the future, restricting Polish initiative.

This state of indecision was based on the belief that a counter-revolution in Russia would be successful. The great powers treated Bolshevism as a political movement similar to other Russian partisan activities. Overrating the potential of Russian counterrevolutionary armies, they expected the rapid downfall of the Bolsheviks as a result of inner struggles and foresaw the restoration of the Romanov dynasty or at least the advent of a new conservative or liberal regime in Russia.

The prevailing opinion in Poland was that the Bolshevik regime would survive the civil war, maintain itself in power, and, after the defeat of its domestic enemies, battle with the West via Poland. The Red Government clearly announced this in a statement published forty-eight hours after the capitulation of Germany. It left no doubt whatever as to the Bolsheviks' intention to transform the whole of Central Europe into a union of Communist states.[26] The demarcation of an internationally recognized Russo-Polish frontier was, therefore, of utmost importance and urgency.

However, there were two different opinions in Poland on how far east the borders of the Polish state should stretch. One was based on the principle that Poland's claims to the east should be restricted to territories where the Polish population was still holding its ground and where the fact of possession would be reinforced by the will of the majority. Thus a relatively small territorial extension would lead to a rapid amalgamation of the Polish state. The National Democrats were partisans of this doctrine, called the theory of incorporation.

The other, the so-called federalist concept, was indirectly based on ancient Polish traditions and on acceptance in the fullest sense of self-determination, the principle advanced under American influence as a basic axiom of the Peace Conference. A number of independent states would be formed by the nations along the territory that was ethnographically pure Russian, from the Ukraine in the south through White Ruthenia (Byelorussia) and Lithuania to the Baltic states in the north. It was presumed that the populaces of these states, having to decide between joining the neighboring Communist Russian state or living independently in association with Poland, would choose the latter alternative. The federalist doctrine, supported by Pilsudski and the leftist groups in the Polish Parliament, appealed to the sentiments of the Polish people. It gained the strong support of the center parties, too, and was dominant for a time, in spite of the National Democrats' opposition.

Notwithstanding its respect for the decisions of the Peace Conference and its gratitude for the Allies' help in restoring its independence, Poland could not afford to risk invasion by the Red Army while waiting for international decisions. The geographic position of the country made it vulnerable to attacks from the east through the so-called White Ruthenian Gate and through the Volhynian Gate. The former opens a passage from Minsk to the southwest toward Bialystok and Warsaw; the latter leads toward the capital by a longer way through the watershed between the Dniester and the Pripet. The primary prerequisite for Poland's security was the possession of a frontier line closing these two routes of access and linking the two important defensive positions, whose centers were Vilna in the north and Lwów in the south.

With the small army, Pilsudski hastened first to bar access to Poland through the northeastern entrance, and pushed the Bolsheviks back step by step. By April, 1919, Vilna was taken. By the end of 1919, the front between the Polish and Russian armies ran roughly 100 miles east of the frontier to be agreed upon later in the Treaty of Riga. After the occupation of Vilna, Pilsudski, in a proclamation dated April 22, promised the inhabitants a civil administration that would provide for self-determination.[27] He reestablished the University of Vilna, founded in 1579 by King Stefan Báthori, and gave substantial help to the starving city. Law and order were reinstated, and economic rehabilitation was begun. Not even Lloyd George could condemn the deliverance of Vilna and its province from the Bolsheviks.

Simultaneously, the struggle between Poles and Ukrainians in eastern Galicia, discussed earlier, was coming to an end; in 1919, the Peace Conference confirmed Polish administration of this province.

After the settlement of those two most pressing problems, the moment to implement the federalist doctrine seemed at hand. A friendly cooperation with the Baltic states had already been initiated. The Polish Army had handed over to Latvia the town and province of Dvinsk (Dunaburg), liberated from the Reds. The Polish Government had taken steps toward an understanding with Lithuania, believing that the two nations, which had been ruled by the same dynasties since 1386 and had been federated in a single commonwealth in 1569, should now enter into a mutual collaboration, especially in the face of their common danger of Bolshevik invasion. But the interests of Poland and Lithuania collided over Vilna. The Lithuanians claimed the province because Vilna had been the capital of the historic Grand Duchy of Lithuania, while the unquestionably Polish character of the province and of the town in particular made it impossible for Poland to give up her rights to it.

The events and negotiations in Polish-Lithuanian relations from 1919 till 1923 were intimately connected with Poland's struggle for her eastern frontiers. However, they must be treated separately as they involve the relations of Poland with a country that had already emancipated itself from foreign rule and had become an independent state. This was not the case of either White Ruthenia or the Ukraine.

In Byelorussia, the national consciousness was weak. This province had belonged to the Grand Duchy of Lithuania in the fourteenth century, and the two subsequently became part of the Polish Commonwealth under the Pact of 1569. Polish claims to Byelorussia, or at least to those parts where Poles constituted a relative majority, were based not only on strategic, economic, and historic arguments, but also on the conviction that to sever those lands from Poland would be to abandon them to the tyranny of Communism.

The Ukrainian question was the most complicated and eventually caused the most serious difficulties in Poland's struggle for the settlement of her eastern frontiers. Since the end of 1917, the situation in the Ukraine, with Kiev as its center, had been confused. An independence movement had started there as a result of the Russian Revolution, and a Ukrainian Republic had been proclaimed in January of the following year. But the Germans, who still occupied the Ukraine, soon replaced the Ukrainian Central Council with their own creation, with "Hetman" Skoropadsky at its head. This regime ended with the defeat of Germany, and a period of chaos followed. Red troops and the "White" army of General Denikin successively occupied Kiev. The Ukrainians endeavored to establish cooperation with the White army, but Denikin refused to negotiate with "traitors to Russia." Denikin was soon defeated, and the Reds occupied almost the whole Ukraine. A split occurred then in the Ukrainian governing body. Semen Petlyura, who was acting as War Minister and Commander in Chief, proclaimed himself dictator and continued to fight at the head of a small nationalist army. In December, 1919, he went to Poland and asked Pilsudski for support against the Bolsheviks. At the same time, he renounced all Ukrainian claims to eastern Galicia and to the western districts of Volhynia.

The idea of cooperating with Petlyura in establishing an independent and friendly Ukraine was favorably considered by the Polish federalists. They thought that a Ukrainian state, even though legally and politically independent, would pursue a policy of friendship and association with Poland because of the menace of Russia's imperialism and her intention to reconquer the rich Ukrainian lands. But advocates of the doctrine of incorporation opposed this view. They had serious doubts as to the degree of national consciousness among the Ukrainian masses and believed that the help of Polish arms in establishing Ukrainian independence would create a lasting antagonism between Russia and Poland.

Before any decision could be taken, a new phase in Soviet-Polish relations opened, on January 28, 1920, with a peace proposal addressed to the Polish Government and signed by Lenin, Trotsky, and Chicherin.[28] In this document, the Soviet Government recognized without reservation the sovereignty and independence of Poland and proposed peace negotiations. It gave assurance that the Red armies would not cross the existing line of the White Ruthenian front—running from Dryssa and Polotsk in the north to Bar in the south—and declared that "insofar as the real interests of Poland and Russia are concerned, there is no single question . . . which could not be decided in a peaceful way."

The Polish Government had good reasons for distrusting the sincerity of this peace offer. Scarcely a year had passed since the Bolshevik armies had swept westward and invaded Polish territory. Now, when the Russians' military operations had taken an unfavorable turn, they proposed peace negotiations. Meanwhile, new Red divisions were arriving at the front.[29] The arrests of Poles as hostages in Russia and the continuing anti-Polish propaganda further strengthened the suspicion that the real aim of the peace proposal was to gain time for military preparations and meanwhile undermine the morale of the Polish people.

The well-informed American envoy in Warsaw, Hugh Gibson, clearly perceived from his conversations with members of the Polish Government, especially Pilsudski, the state of mind of the Poles.[30] He reported to the State Department that the Polish Government, although distrusting the Bolshevik peace offer, had at first considered the necessity of negotiating. But now, he noted, Poland was aware that signing a treaty with Soviet Russia, given the bad faith repeatedly shown by the Bolsheviks, would not liberate Poland from the necessity of maintaining a large army on her eastern borders out of fear of an attack at any time. The morale of the troops would suffer from such a "cold war," and

Communist propaganda emanating from across the border could become dangerously effective.

Pilsudski was convinced of the insincerity of the Soviet move. When the Commission of Foreign Affairs of the Polish Parliament recommended acceptance of peace negotiations, he agreed to give a favorable answer to the Soviet Government. But he decided to consult first with the Western powers, feeling that Poland, placed across the path of world revolution, was entitled in this hour of decision to her allies' advice and to their active support should she be attacked anew by the Red Army.

Stanislaw Patek, Paderewski's successor as Minister of Foreign Affairs, went to Paris and London.[31] At the same time, an exchange of views and information was taking place between Warsaw and Washington. Patek's journey and the Polish Government's efforts to obtain information on the attitude of the Western powers also stemmed from Pilsudski's apprehension that Poland, drawn into armistice and peace negotiations, might be forced to break with England and France, both at that time strongly backing "White" movements in Russia. He believed that the favorable solution of unsettled Polish problems, dependent on the good will of the great powers, would be jeopardized by an independent Polish policy toward Russia. But the Western powers persisted in their state of indecision. Great Britain expressed the opinion that it was up to Poland to decide whether she should negotiate and declined to make any specific promises of assistance.[32] The French Government seemed to encourage Poland not to stop her military activities. After a month of consultations, the Supreme Council issued an enigmatic and highly disappointing declaration on February 24, 1920. It notified "the communities bordering on Russia" that the Allies "were unable to take the responsibility of advising further prosecution of the war, as it might be harmful to their [those communities'] interests. Nor could they advise any aggressive policy toward Russia. If however Russia attacked their legitimate frontiers, the Allies would give them every assistance."[33]

In spite of this unresponsive statement, the Polish Government tried again, in March, 1920, to obtain agreement by the Western powers to a constructive plan for a political order in Eastern

Europe. It suggested creation of a Ukrainian and a Lithuanian–White Ruthenian state along the eastern border of Poland, giving the local populations an opportunity to express their will freely in conformity with the principle of self-determination. At the same time, on March 27, Patek sent Moscow an answer to the peace proposal, suggesting the town of Borysow as the meeting place for the delegations. Chicherin objected that Borysow was situated too near the front line. A long correspondence ensued, both sides maintaining their points of view. Warsaw was unyielding because by April she no longer felt any doubt as to the true intentions of the Bolsheviks. Reliable information had disclosed the concentration of important Soviet troops in the northern sector of the front near Borysow.

After continued Soviet refusal, the Polish Parliament authorized Pilsudski to conclude an agreement with Petlyura.[34] It was signed on April 23, 1920, and three days later Polish troops, led by Pilsudski, started the offensive on the southern front in cooperation with Petlyura's Ukrainian forces. Within a fortnight, they had reached the Dnieper, and they captured Kiev on May 8.

In analyzing Pilsudski's decision to launch the attack on the southern sector of the front when information about the concentration of Red troops in the region of Borysow was already in the possession of the Polish High Command, the political situation must be taken into account. Establishment of an independent and friendly Ukrainian state was the main point of the Polish federalists' plan for settlement of the eastern boundaries of Poland. Petlyura was seeking Polish help to liberate the Ukraine from Russia, and there were serious arguments in favor of lending him support. He had maintained himself at the helm of the independence movement longer than any other Ukrainian leader; he had obtained active and substantial help from the Allies; and he was expecting and promising a general uprising of the Ukrainians against the Bolsheviks. Pilsudski felt that a refusal to grant the aid requested by a nation that had lived in union with Poland for 400 years would be a stain on Polish honor.

There was no doubt whatever—and not even Pilsudski's strongest opponents in Poland claimed there was—that Pilsudski's concept of liberating the White Ruthenians and the Ukrainians, two branches of eastern Slavdom, was based on the old Polish revolutionary slogan "For your freedom and ours." He never planned to incorporate these lands into Poland. Proof of his true intentions can be found in his proclamation to the Ukrainians, in which he stated that Polish troops would remain in the Ukraine only until the Ukrainians, having constituted their lawful government, were able to organize the defense of their country by themselves.[35]

The Bolsheviks had a federation program of their own, but, in conformity with their creed and principles, those supposedly "federated" nations were to be only parts of a rigidly united system of Communist-ruled local governments, completely subject to Moscow. The Polish federalists hoped that the Ukrainians would unhesitatingly join forces with the Polish Army for liberation from their Bolshevik oppressors.

But despite the friendly attitude of the people, it soon became clear that Petlyura was deluding himself when he hoped for a general patriotic uprising in the Ukraine. His appeals mustered only negligible forces, and it was apparent that the Poles could not carry on the fight with such weak support. The small army that had initiated the offensive had to occupy considerable areas, and, with the extension of the front line, communications with the rear became increasingly difficult. At the same time, the Polish attack had enabled the Bolsheviks to stimulate the patriotic feelings of the Russians. Thousands of "White" officers, with General Brusilov at their head, offered their services to the Communists.[36] Moreover, only a few days after the Poles occupied Kiev, strong Bolshevik forces launched a sudden attack on the most dangerous sector in the north, breaking through the Polish line between the Dvina and Beresina rivers. Under the impact of this Soviet offensive, Polish troops were forced to retreat hastily along the whole front line and could not make a stand until the Red armies had pushed almost to the outskirts of Warsaw. The Polish military situation looked almost hopeless. It seemed certain that within a few weeks, or even days, Poland would be overrun by the Bolsheviks, opening up the road for a Red advance into Central Europe.

And extension of Communism into Germany would, in turn, open unlimited prospects for revolutionary movements in vast areas of Europe.

This was the opinion of the political leaders of Poland; accordingly, they took every possible measure to mobilize the nation's moral and material resources.[37] They appealed to the West for help and support in a struggle that they considered to be in the common interest.

At that very time, the Supreme Council had convened in the Belgian resort of Spa to discuss certain reparations questions. The Polish Government seized the opportunity and submitted to the Allies an urgent request for political and material support. Prime Minister Wladyslaw Grabski, a distinguished economist, headed the Polish delegation.

In Spa the Poles found themselves in a difficult position, several factors having rendered their cause unpopular. The Western Allies were still hoping for a victory of the anti-Communist nationalist forces in Russia, toward whom they felt a moral obligation because of Russia's participation in the initial phase of World War I. Many considered the advance of the Polish Army into Russia an imperialist campaign. Public opinion in Western Europe, desiring the re-establishment of peace everywhere, accused Poland of warlike tendencies. Moreover, the new Polish state lacked experience; it did not have adequate instruments abroad for disseminating information to explain the problems involved and correct prejudiced opinions.[38] The Poles received in Spa much criticism and little help from the assembled statesmen; Lloyd George, whose opinions prevailed in the negotiations, was no more friendly than he had been at Paris. The French representative, Millerand, in spite of his sympathy for Poland and the opinions of the French military advisers, remained aloof because of the need for British good will and cooperation in the reparations question.[39] Thus Grabski, arriving at Spa when it seemed that the capital of Poland would be taken by the Red Army within days, was at a severe disadvantage.

Grabski was able to obtain from the Supreme Council a promise of help and mediation for Poland, but only by accepting highly onerous conditions. Some of them—those concerning Lithuania, Danzig, and Teschen—later had an important bearing on Poland's foreign policy. Poland lived up to the imposed conditions so far as possible, agreeing to a peace conference as required, but the promise of help was never fulfilled. The British Government, in particular, did not abide by its pledge "to assist the Polish nation to defend its existence with all the means at their disposal," even after the Soviet Government[40] rejected the Curzon proposals.

Fortunately, the Polish nation, aware of the disaster that victorious Communism could mean for Poland and of its danger to the whole of Europe, mobilized all its moral and material forces to throw back the Russian advance. The battle for the bridgehead of Warsaw, in which the Red Army was defeated and forced to retreat, turned the tide. The Poles fought without help except for General Weygand's French military mission.[41] Actual hindrance came from Danzig, Germany, and the Czechs, who refused to grant the necessary transit permissions for military supplies. Thus the victory was won almost entirely by what a British historian has described as the soaring of "the national spirit . . . to wonderful heights of devotion and self-sacrifice."

Meanwhile, as an armistice proposal sent to Moscow by the Polish Government had been accepted, a Polish delegation, headed by Undersecretary of State Dabski left for Minsk, arriving two days before the decisive battle of Warsaw. Kept practically interned, they had no information that the Red Army was in full retreat and learned by mere chance about the complete reversal of the military situation. As the peace conditions offered by the Russians were unacceptable, they rejected them and protested strongly against the treatment to which they were subjected.

The rapid advance of the Polish Army made Russia more inclined to seek a compromise. It was decided to transfer the negotiations to a neutral capital and Riga was chosen as the site. Preliminary peace conditions and an armistice agreement were signed on October 12, 1920, whereupon military operations were suspended. One month later, peace negotiations were resumed, lasting until March 18, 1921, when the Treaty of Riga was signed.[42] Both parties considered that, having made sacrifices in the interest of peaceful neighborly relations, they had attained a satisfactory solution of all pending problems. Poland renounced her federation plans, and Soviet Russia declared her disinterest in the Polish-Lithuanian problem.[43] The frontier line agreed upon coincided roughly with that of the second partition of Poland in 1793. It was a reasonable compromise based, as much as possible in a borderland with mixed populations, on fair geographic estimates.

The Treaty of Riga marked the end of the arduous military and political struggle for settlement of Poland's eastern frontier. Two years elapsed, however, before the Riga frontier was internationally recognized. Only on March 14, 1923, did the Conference of Ambassadors decide to confirm Poland's sovereign rights over the areas defined by the Treaty.

II

The Shaping of Foreign Policy: 1921–26

FOR FIVE YEARS after Poland had regained her independence and begun to rebuild her state, Polish foreign policy was, in a large measure, dependent on the Central and East European conditions arising from wartime destruction and disorganization. The attitudes and policies of the victorious Entente powers also had to be taken into account. Poland had hoped for help from the great powers in the solution of her urgent problems. These countries, however, wrestling with problems of the highest magnitude and beset by conflicting interests, did not rank Poland high among their recognized responsibilities. Thus, the Polish Government had to adapt foreign-policy decisions to each particular situation or problem. Only gradually could governing principles of foreign policy emerge and long-range planning take place.

Paderewski—virtually the first Foreign Minister—had the arduous task, along with Dmowski, of representing Polish interests at the Paris Peace Conference, where nebulous and often impracticable concepts concerning Eastern and Central Europe prevailed. His successors, Patek and Sapieha, had to defend Poland's rights and claims under the still more difficult conditions of actual war with Soviet Russia and unfriendly acts by other neighbors. The three succeeding heads of the Foreign Ministry—Skirmunt, Narutowicz, and Skrzynski—were in a better position, formulating foreign policy under conditions of established peace on the frontiers, and therefore with more independence from military events and with greater authority. However, they were faced with difficulties inherent in the structure of Polish parliamentarianism, which was based on the progressive French system and carried democratic ideas to the extreme.

Party strife, with its bargaining for positions and influence in the government, created political instability in the domestic sphere; frequent cabinet changes retarded the development of a consistent and well-defined foreign policy. The hasty democratization of the people, the majority of whom had been denied any participation in political activities for several generations, further differentiated and fractionalized the political parties. The formation of a united majority in the government became difficult. Neither the Right, with the National Democrats at its head, nor the Left, led by the Socialist Party, was strong enough to form a stable government.

Legislative power was made preponderant by the Constitution of March 17, 1921, which established a clear-cut supremacy of parliament over the executive branch of government.[1] This brought about serious governmental crises that lasted as long as several weeks. The weaknesses of the parliamentary regime were further aggravated by the precarious economic and financial situation. After 150 years of foreign rule, the country had failed to develop most of the economic assets that the industrial progress of the nineteenth century had brought to much of Europe. None of the three partitioning powers had made investments in Poland; industrialization was insufficient for the needs of a modern state; the network of highways, railroads, and waterways was inadequate; and there were too few public buildings, schools, and hospitals. War devastation was greater in Poland than in any other country in Central Europe. The Central powers and Russia had waged battle over some 75 per cent of the Polish territory, with the front shifting backward and forward. The Russo-Polish war had so ravaged the land that it had created an appalling shortage of food and other supplies; famine was avoided mainly through the prompt and generous action of the United States.[2]

Inflation, resulting from devaluation of the currencies inherited from the occupying powers and expenditures in the war with Soviet Russia, produced a devastating effect on the economy. The peak of inflation was reached in 1923, when the catastrophic devaluation of the German mark so affected Polish currency that it ceased to perform its normal economic function. This critical situation led to the formation of a cabinet of experts, unhampered by party strife, with Grabski as Prime Minister and Minister of Finance. Having obtained extensive powers in financial matters from the Seym, Grabski introduced a new legal tender, the zloty, and undertook far-reaching financial reforms that put an end to the inflation.

But the upward turn in the economic and financial area did not clearly stabilize the political sector. Party antagonism remained intense and again provoked changes of cabinets. During that period (1923–26), the Ministry of Foreign Affairs was headed in turn by Seyda, Dmowski, Zamoyski, and Skrzynski (who had previously held that position from December, 1922, to May, 1923). A fall of the new currency in 1925, in connection with Germany's prohibition of imports of Polish coal, undermined public confidence in the parliamentary regime and increased the general feeling of disappointment. The growing unrest, the dissatisfaction of the working classes, and the negative attitude of the Socialist Party led to still another governmental crisis in May, 1926, followed by the *coup d'état* of Marshal Pilsudski.

Pilsudski, who in 1921 had refused to become a candidate for the Presidency of the Republic, had left the army in 1923 and retired from active politics. His decision to re-enter politics was based on his estimate that the general internal situation—a situation he personally had contributed to by his vehement and unremitting attacks on the parliamentary factions—was likely to provoke a popular outburst. The *coup d'état* of May, 1926, was not merely a military rebellion. Supported by the well-organized Socialist Party, it had a political objective. It sought to strengthen the executive power, and it led to a decline in the importance of political parties.

Under the new regime, Pilsudski was nominally just a member of the cabinet; actually he was—and remained until his death—the leading power behind the Government.[3] He scrupulously avoided any steps calculated to destroy either the Parliament or the Constitution, but no decision of importance was taken without his approval, particularly in foreign policy and defense. As a rule, he did not interfere in the administration of the state, but he regarded military and international affairs as his exclusive domain. From May, 1926, onward, Poland's foreign policy was guided by Pilsudski.

Although the successive Ministers of Foreign Affairs preceding the *coup d'état* of 1926 were men of various political opinions and party affiliations, the main lines of Poland's international endeavors remained unchanged. However deeply the Poles were divided on questions of domestic policy, the majority of the people approved the direction foreign policy took after the end of the war with Russia and the conclusion of the Riga Treaty.

The principal aim of Polish foreign policy was to create a political system that would permit Poland to develop her national life in peace and security. Such a policy had to be based on an adequate system of alliances and on cooperation with all peaceful nations within the League of Nations, which served as an instrument for European stability. Because the Treaty of Versailles, which had re-established peace between Germany and the Allied nations, had also become the political and legal foundation of Poland's independence, Poland was definitely tied to the territorial order created by that treaty. France, the great power most interested in maintaining this order, was the natural ally of Poland, and a formal alliance between the two countries would be a deterrent to German endeavors at revenge. In addition, the ever-present danger of Russian imperialism induced Poland to seek cooperation with nations similarly menaced. Hence the early collaboration with Rumania and the endeavor to create a community of views and interests with the Baltic states.

After driving back the Soviet armies and settling her eastern frontiers, Poland became, in the opinion of the West and particularly of France, an ally on the side of peace and order. The defeat of the various restoration movements in Russia and the apparent permanence of the Soviet regime had put an end to the hope that that country could resume its role in the French system of alliances—at least for a number of years. In recognition of Poland's role in checking the advance of Bolshevism in Europe, the French Government decided to establish closer political links with Poland and extended an invitation to Pilsudski to come to Paris. The

Marshal—in the company of the Foreign Minister, Prince Sapieha, and the Minister of Military Affairs, General Sosnkowski—paid a state visit to France. A Franco-Polish political agreement, virtually a treaty of alliance, was signed. Two days later, a military convention was concluded, providing for mutual assistance in case of unprovoked German attack and for French help to Poland in case of aggression by Soviet Russia. Those agreements—despite various periods of dissension or misunderstanding—remained the cornerstone of Polish foreign policy until the outbreak of World War II, and they provided the legal and political foundation for the French declaration of war on Germany in September, 1939. They continued in force until both nations were invaded and lost their freedom in World War II.[4]

The Franco-Polish alliance was the first of a series of agreements with which Poland sought to protect herself from Germany and Russia. If the main purpose of the agreement with France was to hold Germany in check, the objective of Poland's next move was to provide a safeguard against Russian aggression.

On March 3, 1921, a defensive alliance with Rumania was signed by Foreign Minister Sapieha in Bucharest. Rumania, even more than Poland, was interested in close collaboration between the two countries. Whereas Russo-Polish territorial problems had been settled in the Treaty of Riga, Rumania's annexation of Bessarabia had never been agreed to by Russia and could serve as a pretext for aggression.[5] From their inception in 1919, relations between Poland and Rumania had been characterized by complete understanding and cordiality. Even during the Peace Conference in Paris, the distinguished Rumanian statesman Take Yonescu had begun talks with Polish leaders about a future collaboration. The Convention for a Defensive Alliance of 1921, a logical conclusion of earlier contacts and negotiations, provided for mutual assistance in case of unprovoked attack on their eastern frontiers. Renewed periodically, it was extended to 1941. The alliance with Rumania brought Poland the advantage of a safe and friendly relationship with the largest and potentially most prosperous nation of southeastern Europe. Its importance for both signatories was underscored during an exchange of state visits by Pilsudski and the King of Rumania in 1922 and 1923, as well as during other visits of political and military leaders in succeeding years.

At the time the Polish-Rumanian alliance was concluded, the nucleus of what later became a regional organization—the Little Entente—was already in existence. A Czechoslovak-Yugoslav mutual-defense pact concluded on August 14, 1920, initiated close cooperation among the neighbors of Hungary, and the attempt—in March, 1920, in Budapest—to restore the Hapsburg dynasty accelerated realization of this scheme. True, Take Yonescu had conceived of a different regional arrangement in 1918, when he first discussed with Dmowski and Benes the necessity for a closely knit belt of states between Germany and Russia from the Baltic to the Aegean Sea. Actually, this vast plan was reduced to a grouping of Czechoslovakia, Yugoslavia, and Rumania with the limited aim of enforcing the Treaty of Trianon on Hungary and checking her revisionism.

On various occasions—for example, at the Conference of Genoa in 1922—Poland collaborated closely with the Little Entente. But in spite of the common platform of antirevisionism and the similarity of their relations with France, Poland remained outside the organization. The traditional Polish-Hungarian friendship was a major reason for Poland's reluctance to join it. Another was the opposition of Czechoslovakia—whose role in the Little Entente had been a dominant one from the start—and the continued Polish resentment over Czechoslovakia's effective seizure of a large part of Teschen during Poland's life-or-death struggle with Russia.

The idea of an entente between Poland and the small Baltic states took shape in the early 1920's. It was based on the similar political situations of all the countries bordering Russia that had won their independence after the downfall of the Czarist monarchy. The threat of the expansion of Russian Communism was an incentive for solidarity and cooperation among them.

Initial steps in that direction were taken in 1919, but in the following year the fear of a Soviet victory over Poland as well as the Polish-Lithuanian conflict prevented further advance. An active Polish policy aiming at the realization of a Baltic League began only in March, 1922, at a conference of the foreign ministers of Estonia, Finland, Latvia, and Poland, held in Warsaw. The ministers signed a political convention providing for friendly co-operation between the four states in case of an unprovoked attack against any one of them. However, Finland did not ratify the agreement, and thus the convention did not take effect. Nevertheless, further conferences among the foreign ministers of the four states followed. Although these contributed to the development of friendly relations, the establishment of a Baltic League was not attained. In addition to Finland's refusal to cooperate, a number of other factors contributed to this failure: Germany and Russia, each for its own reasons, used various means to counteract and nullify Poland's efforts to increase her influence in the Baltic area; the Western powers were, at best, indifferent to the plans for Baltic integration; and, the most important obstacle of all, Lithuania was opposed to any collaboration with Poland.

The Polish-Lithuanian controversy was of a peculiar nature and unprecedented intricacy. The problem centered—as stated above—upon the possession of Vilna. Poland's claim rested on ethnographical factors, Lithuania's on historical considerations. If Poland's title to Vilna rested on the large numerical preponderance of Poles over Lithuanians, the importance Poland attached to her claim derived also from the strategic value of this region for defense against attacks from the east and for direct connection between Poland and Latvia. It was for these reasons that Germany and Russia—both equally interested in preventing the penetration of Polish influence into the Baltic region—repeatedly gave their support to the Lithuanian claims.

In 1917–18, the Germans had sponsored the creation of a Lithuanian Council and later of a Lithuanian Government with its capital in Vilna. The presence of Lithuanian political bodies in that city led to constant conflict between the government and the local population and, at the time of the German retreat, to Polish-Lithuanian controversy over the Polish proposal for a common defense of Vilna against the Red Army. In consequence, the Lithuanian Government was transferred to Kaunas, and the city of Vilna was occupied for a short time by the Bolsheviks. Liberated by Polish troops in April, 1919, it was again invaded by the

Russians during their successful campaign of 1920. This time, the Soviet Government took the opportunity to promote Lithuanian territorial claims. In a treaty concluded on July 12, 1920, it conceded to the Lithuanians not only the region and the city of Vilna, but all the territories Lithuania had ever claimed, even those over which Polish administration had been extended in accordance with the Supreme Council's specific authorization.

Although Lithuania had declared her neutrality in the Russo-Polish conflict, the Soviet Government obtained, on the occasion of the signing of the treaty, secret assurance that the Lithuanian Government would allow soldiers of the Red Army to pass freely through its territory.[6] Such a secret arrangement was in itself a violation of Lithuania's neutrality; the subsequent retreat of the Soviet armies was an even more flagrant violation. Thousands of Russian soldiers who had crossed the East Prussian frontier were allowed to pass through Lithuanian territory and join the regrouping Soviet Army. At the same time, the presence of supposedly neutral Lithuanian forces in areas where military operations continued hampered the freedom of action of the Poles and was used to the advantage of the Soviet Army. To protect Polish interests under these complicated conditions, the Polish Government appealed to the League of Nations, protesting the Lithuanian violation of neutrality laws. The Council of the League of Nations began international proceedings by appointing a Control Commission, whose endeavors contributed greatly to the elimination of armed clashes. It also took part in the direct negotiations of the parties at Suwalki, which led finally to the acceptance of a provisional demarcation line. But before this agreement came into force, the occupation of Vilna by General Zeligowski changed the situation completely.

The Polish General Lucjan Zeligowski, a native of Vilna and head of a division composed of citizens of the Vilna region, allegedly rebelled, seized the city, and established a local government over the area, which he called Central Lithuania.[7] In a proclamation to the population, he stated that he was acting in their name and interest and that he did not expect any help from

Poland, bound as Poland was by obligations to the Western powers.

Lithuania immediately appealed to the League of Nations. With the help of the Control Commission, negotiations between Zeligowski and the Lithuanians were begun, and a provisional solution was reached that created a neutral zone dividing Central Lithuania from Lithuania proper. In this way, the military phase of the *coup* was brought to a close.

Lithuanian-Polish negotiations were begun next under the auspices of the League of Nations, with the Belgian Foreign Minister, Paul Hymans, acting as chairman of the conference. After almost a year, no agreement was reached; it was only demonstrated that the crux of the problem lay in the Lithuanians' firm decision not to admit any constitutional link or closer cooperation with Poland—a solution Pilsudski was seeking to impose. No understanding was possible under such circumstances.

To satisfy the promise made to the people of Vilna, elections for a Constituent Assembly were held in the presence of the League of Nations Control Commission in January, 1922. The overwhelming majority of the 106 delegates voted for the immediate reunion of Vilna with the Polish Republic. After certain difficulties on the part of Pilsudski, who still hoped for some kind of compromise with Lithuania over Vilna, the town and district were incorporated into Poland by a decision of the Polish Seym. A few days later, the Vilna Assembly was dissolved.

In January, 1923, the Lithuanian occupation of the territory of Memel by force emphasized the necessity for an international decision on the territorial problems involved. The Polish Government made use of the opportunity to begin vigorous diplomatic action to secure the agreement of the Conference of Ambassadors to the territorial *status quo* in the east. Lithuania also requested that the Allied powers make use of their rights to fix Poland's eastern frontier. Poland met with success. On March 15, 1923, the Conference of Ambassadors rendered a decision accepting the Riga Treaty line as the frontier between Russia and Poland.[8] The Polish-Lithuanian frontier, described in detail in the same decision, corresponded to the demarcation line previously agreed upon.

Lithuania did not accept the decision, and attempted, though unsuccessfully, to prolong negotiations. A situation arose in which no diplomatic relations whatsoever existed between the two neighboring countries, and Lithuania considered herself to be in a state of war with Poland.

Another effort to undermine the settlement of the eastern problems came from Russia. On April 5, the Commissar for Foreign Affairs, Chicherin, sent a note to the Government of Poland protesting the intervention of the great powers in the question of the Polish-Lithuanian frontier. Such a move was in line with Moscow's general policy—a consistent endeavor to foment controversies and to prevent closer collaboration between Poland and the Baltic states. Relations between Poland and Russia were far from cordial at that time, despite the praise for the compromise of Riga expressed in the final speeches of the chairmen of both peace delegations.[9] Poland's acceptance of the Treaty of Riga as the solution to the conflict was genuine and sincere; Russia, contrary to opinions current in the West, did not resent the territorial arrangements resulting from the treaty. Official Soviet sources admitted that Poland had obtained a less advantageous frontier than the one the Soviets had proposed and were ready to concede to her in January, 1920. But the defeat of the Red Army in 1920 was unquestionably a blow to the pride of revolutionary Russia. The Polish victory had also checked the advance of Communism at a moment when revolutionary movements in Germany and the temporary realization of Communist rule in Hungary seemed to promise further Communist expansion in Europe. In spite of clear demonstrations that, in her struggle with Russia, Poland had obtained little help from the Allies and was not playing the role of "watchdog" or "policeman" of Europe, the Soviets remained highly suspicious of every connection between Poland and the West. In Poland's collaboration with France, Great Britain, and the United States, Russia was inclined to see the menace of a coalition capable of armed intervention against Bolshevism. This specter of a *cordon sanitaire* exerted its detrimental influence on normal Soviet-Polish relations for a long period. Still, even when relations were extremely strained, Russia was careful to avoid a diplomatic break. Warsaw represented a valuable observation post for Soviet diplomacy, especially during periods of Russian isolation.

This troubled background to Soviet-Polish relations accounts for the many difficulties that arose over the execution of the Treaty of Riga. The Soviet Government evinced such a degree of ill will in carrying out its stipulations that only a small part of them were fully executed. Poland's reactions were confined to conventional diplomatic actions at first. Konstanty Skirmunt, Foreign Minister from June, 1921, to June, 1922, chose the tactics of persuasion and even concession. His previous diplomatic successes, obtained mostly through notable tact and straightforwardness, induced him to employ similar methods toward Soviet Russia. He believed that in this way he would gain Russia's cooperation and the approval of France and Great Britain.

Yielding to Soviet complaints, the Polish Government agreed to turn out the group of Russian emigrees led by Savinkoff who were accused of anti-Soviet activities. Another proof of Poland's good will was the invitation extended to the Soviet Government to attend a conference of the Baltic states convened in Warsaw to establish a common policy for the International Conference of Genoa. At approximately the same time, Skirmunt sent delegates to Berlin for confidential discussions with the Soviet agents Krestinsky and Radek concerning the possibilities of a better understanding between France and Russia.[10] All Polish conciliatory moves, no matter how disinterested, were interpreted by Moscow as signs of weakness. Soviet propaganda and diplomatic activities were aimed at preventing the strengthening of ties between Poland and the Baltic states, and the Communists deliberately maintained a state of unrest along the whole eastern border of Poland. Communist emissaries of propaganda were smuggled across the frontier, and raids were carried out on Polish territory by bands of armed men. Several of these incursions were undertaken by groups so large that no doubt could exist that such attacks were organized on Russian territory with the knowledge of Soviet authorities.[11]

At the end of 1922, recognizing the failure of efforts to improve Polish-Soviet relations by a policy of appeasement and patience, Poland abandoned all attempts at unilateral concessions. She took vigorous measures to bring quiet to the frontier area and to protect the local population. Toward this end, a frontier guard, the Corps of Frontier Protection, was formed in 1924 and placed under the orders of the Minister of the Interior. It soon put an end to the incursions of lawless bands and contributed greatly to the return of normal conditions along the eastern frontier.

Despite the numerous difficulties encountered by Poland in establishing neighborly relations with the Soviet Union in accordance with the Treaty of Riga's "final, lasting, and honorable peace based on mutual understanding," some improvement was reached in the negotiation of minor and technical, though important, problems. Agreements were concluded that regulated freight and passenger travel on the railway lines between Warsaw and Moscow and set up a sanitary convention and a postal and telegraphic arrangement. This gradual resumption of normal Russo-Polish relations paralleled the decline of Soviet leaders' hopes for revolutionary upheavals that would spread Communism beyond the borders of Russia. On the whole, in the mid-1920's, the relations between Russia and her western neighbors were satisfactory. Soviet initiative resulted in the conclusion of agreements that aimed at the reinforcement of peace and security in that part of Europe. Poland, for her part, contributed readily to the development of a system of nonaggression pacts with the Soviet Union, insisting on the simultaneous conclusion of pertinent agreements with all the states bordering Russia on the west. Thus some solidarity developed among the western neighbors of Russia in spite of the failure of plans for a more integrated Baltic League.

In her relations with the Soviet Union, Poland had to deal with an ethical, social, and economic system fundamentally different from her own. In her relations with Germany, she confronted political purposes and aims diametrically opposed to her own. Poland belonged to the Allied camp, and her foreign policy had to be based on the existing system of peace treaties. Germany, on the other hand, was determined to act in opposition to this system. She had been deprived of territorial conquests and could not reconcile herself to the loss of her Polish provinces. The majority of German political and military leaders, educated in the Bismarckian school, looked upon an independent Poland as a disastrous obstacle to German expansion to the east.

From the time that peace was re-established, Germany carried on a campaign of hostile propaganda to undermine the world's confidence in Poland's viability. Poland was described as a "temporary state" (*Saisonstaat*), and the necessity for a revision of the German-Polish frontier was continuously proclaimed. In order to create difficulties for Poland, the Germans exploited to the utmost all the complicated problems inherent in the liquidation of German rule in Polish territory. The Polish land reform, disputed cases of nationality, transit across Poland to East Prussia—all these problems were treated as grievances by Germany, and all became the subjects of charges against Poland. The provisions of the Treaty of Versailles were in many cases rendered void, and the Germans succeeded more than once in obtaining concessions through protest and litigation carried to the League of Nations and the Permanent Court of International Justice.

There were two fields in particular in which Germany exerted her hostile influence to the detriment of Poland: Danzig and the German minority in Poland.

As discussed above,[12] Poland's vital need for access to the Baltic seaboard had found a complex and unsatisfactory solution in the creation of the Free City of Danzig. The peacemakers' intention to maintain the German character of Danzig and at the same time to assure Poland full use of the port was frustrated. The local government of the city was staffed largely by Prussian officials who acquired Danzig citizenship without losing their German status. Their overwhelming influence, employed to create difficulties between Poland and Danzig, could hardly be opposed by the few native Danzigers in the administration. The welfare of the city depended upon intimate economic links with Poland, as proved by centuries of harmonious relations. But this was subordinated and sacrificed to the political aims of Germany.

The German bias of the Danzig administration found its expression in the negotiations between Poland and Danzig, held under the auspices of the Supreme Council, to settle problems taken up only generally in the Treaty of Versailles. The Danzig delegation, headed by Chief Burgomaster Sahm, made claims that would deprive Poland of important rights granted her in the treaty. Although the Supreme Council rejected these claims and took into account some of the Polish demands, the specific terms of the convention concluded in Paris on November 9, 1920, reflected the tendency to curtail Polish privileges deriving from the spirit and the letter of the treaty. Poland had no choice but to sign it, having undertaken in Spa to abide by the decision of the Supreme Council. As a consequence, the management of the port and its installations, which Poland should have taken over, was handed to the Danzig Port and Waterways Board, composed of representatives of Danzig and Poland in equal numbers, with a neutral chairman. Similarly, the clear stipulation providing for the inclusion of Danzig in Poland's customs area was converted into a complicated system of customs union. Using the various procedures provided for settlement of differences, and particularly the right to appeal to the League of Nations, Poland and Danzig became involved in many disputes (approximately a hundred).[13] The conflict over instituting postal service, amounting to little more than setting up a few mail boxes, is a good example of how the real issue could be and often was obscured in the course of legal processes and laborious negotiation.[14] It served German propaganda to point out the impossibility of maintaining the status of Danzig as part of the Polish economic system.

The paralyzing effects on the economic interests of both Poland and Danzig were undeniable; but the movement of trade in the Free City from 1923 on showed a remarkable increase over the most prosperous years under Prussian rule. The economic revival, however, failed to bring about a change in the hostile attitude of the Danzig authorities toward Poland.

Perhaps the Poles could have reinforced the existing tendency for Danzig to cooperate fully with its natural hinterland had they initially undertaken a serious effort to participate actively in its commercial activities through immigration, investments, and the establishment of enterprises. The influx of Polish capital and the presence of a larger group of enterprising Poles could have initiated a change of mind and policy in Danzig. Unfortunately, the task of reconstruction in Poland occupied the energies of the Poles. Moreover, very soon after the war, the Danzig administration began to oppose any Polish endeavors to take part in the economic life of the city. Neither Polish citizens nor Polish firms could count on nondiscriminatory treatment by the authorities.

The Polish Government and public watched these developments, first with perplexity and later with alarm. The effort and expense incurred in maintaining and expanding the port facilities were not repaid by the cooperation that the growing commerce of Poland required. The lessons of the recent past,[15] the need to secure a safe outlet for Poland's overseas exports, and the necessity of possessing and supplying an adequate naval force led to consideration of a new approach to the question of Poland's access to the sea. The paradoxical fact that Polish merchandise had to be directed to German ports because of Danzig's obstructionist attitude pointed the way to a solution. Poland decided to establish a modern port of its own on the small strip of coast over which she possessed full jurisdiction. Within a few years, Gdynia, a fishermen's village, became a modern port that could handle a sizable part of Poland's commerce. "The second lung of Poland to the sea is breathing, and the Poles are breathing more freely," wrote a contemporary Italian author about this development.[16]

As was to be expected, Danzig, having missed the opportunity to attract the whole maritime commerce of Poland, began proceedings, claiming a right of monopoly to all Polish sea-borne trade. This procedure finally resulted in a Polish-Danzig agreement. A joint committee was created, with the task of adjusting the claims connected with Polish maritime trade.

Contrary to the complaints of Danzig, Gdynia did not "crush Danzig out of existence."[17] The technical development of the port facilities in Danzig and the steadily growing shipment and transshipment of goods by the port were proofs of its vigorous life.

The never-ending squabbles and quarrels between Danzig and Poland were put into proper light in 1934, after the signing of the German-Polish declaration of nonaggression. From that moment on, no Polish-Danzig problem was submitted for decision to the League of Nations, and it became evident that the Free City had been only a pawn in the much more ominous and dangerous area of Polish-German relations.

Germany's revisionist trends appeared also in the German Government's exploitation of the minority problem as an instrument for the achievement of its own goals. In the first place, Germany wanted to stimulate nationalist feelings and activities among the German minority in Poland, making it an efficient tool of Berlin's policy. All complaints submitted by that minority to the League of Nations, many of them groundless or insignificant, were supported by Germany.[18]

From 1921 onward, the German minority in Poland provided favorable ground for the theories of the new science of nationhood developed in Germany—the *Volkstumslehre*—whose promoters advocated a political, economic, and social autonomy for German minorities abroad. The role played by these minorities, especially in countries bordering on Germany, has been adequately evaluated in various studies describing what during World War II was called the "fifth column." The well-organized German communities abroad demanded the privilege that theorists called the *Volksgruppenrecht*, which would enable the minority to disrupt the political integrity of the host nation. This went beyond the purpose of the treaties imposed upon a limited group of Central and East European nations for the protection of minorities—treaties intended merely to assure effective protection of the rights of the individuals who were alien to the majority because of race, creed, or language.

The Germans in Poland, whose number was officially estimated before World War II to be 800,000, possessed several powerful organizations corresponding approximately to the party pattern in Germany. During Hitler's rule, almost all these associations proclaimed their loyalty to National Socialism. Financial support for their activities was provided by German industrialists and landowners of Upper Silesia, Posnania, and Pomerania, whose economic situation reflected the privileged position they had enjoyed before World War I. Moreover, through various devices, the minority organizations also received help from Germany.

The continuous discussion in the Council of the League of Nations of the complaints of these minorities was intended by Germany to demonstrate that the "intolerable" position of the Germans within Poland's frontiers resulted from a territorial situation urgently requiring revision. The memoirs of Gustav Stresemann contain indications that in working for the admission of Germany to the League of Nations, he was aware of the advantage it would give the Reich to have the right, as a member of the Council, to raise questions concerning minority problems. When Germany joined the League in 1926, the petitions and claims of German minorities began to multiply in number, particularly from Upper Silesia.

Germany did not want to establish economic relations with Poland during the first two years after the end of the war. On the contrary, the Germans intended to ruin Poland by economic isolation and pressure, and hoped to demonstrate in this way the temporary nature of the Polish state. The result was that the Poles sought other markets and endeavored to substitute their own products for those they could not obtain from Germany. Becoming aware of the disadvantages of such a situation for her own economy, Germany entered into commercial relations with Poland in 1922 and soon became her most important customer and supplier. However, the Polish Government wished to avoid exclusive dependence on goods from Germany and therefore, in the early 1920's, concluded agreements with several other countries. This led to a reduction of commerce with Germany.

An important item in German-Polish commerce was the duty-free export of Polish coal to Germany, under the Geneva Convention on Upper Silesia of May, 1922. This privilege was to be valid for three years after the conclusion of the Convention.[19] Before its expiration, the German Government informed Poland of the conditions under which it would be willing to grant her an extension—conditions mainly political in character. Among other demands, Germany asked Poland to abandon her treaty rights to former German property and to abrogate the clauses on the eviction of optants. Poland refused these terms, and Germany did not renew permission for the duty-free import of Polish coal. When the Polish Government, in turn, took retaliatory measures, Germany refused to import Polish agricultural products. Another serious financial blow was the withdrawal of German capital from Polish banks. An economic war resulted from all these measures; in spite of repeated negotiations and efforts to redress the situation, it lasted until March, 1934.

Despite the heavy consequences of the tariff war with Germany, which hit when Poland was devaluing the national currency and was already involved in severe economic difficulties, the ruinous crisis foretold by various German sources failed to occur.[20] On the contrary, the threat of such a catastrophe became a stimulus to the Poles to create their own industries, export their own products, and begin a vigorous quest for new markets. Fortunately for the Polish coal industry, the British coal strike of 1926 enabled Poland to export to countries previously dependent on England.

Thus, Poland benefited in the long run from the tariff war by emancipating her economy from the German market, developing her own resources, and establishing commercial connections with other countries. In sum, the gains in this struggle outweighed the losses, which, at the beginning of the tariff war, had seemed to pose a serious threat to Poland's economic existence.

From the political viewpoint, though, the constant tension between Berlin and Warsaw was a very real handicap for Poland, most specifically in her dealings with the League of Nations. Polish public opinion had welcomed the League of Nations Covenant, partly because of its political significance as a part of the Versailles Treaty, and also because its lofty principles corresponded to the ideals professed for generations by the Polish nation. The two major principles of the League—the equality of states, and collective security—had the undivided support of the

Poles, who considered them a guarantee of Poland's rightful place within organized international society. But the delays of the Allied powers in defining the new territorial order in Central and Eastern Europe—particularly regarding Poland—and the decisions introducing special regimes and plebiscites or leaving territorial problems for future settlement were a direct invitation to "intrigue, propaganda, tyranny and terrorism"[21] against Poland. Having to settle pending problems by their own efforts, the Poles inevitably came into conflict with their neighbors and were accused of imperialism and aggression before the Council of the League of Nations. Danzig, Polish-Lithuanian relations, Polish-Czechoslovak disputes, and the German minorities' petitions were recurrent problems submitted to the Council, and Poland became its best "client."[22] The continuous preoccupation with petty questions hindered the Polish Government and its delegates in Geneva from participating fully in more important discussions. From 1920 to 1923, much of the time and effort of the representatives of Poland in Geneva—Paderewski and his successor, Simon Askenazy—was devoted to the tedious and thankless task of defending Poland in minor conflicts. The Polish people found it humiliating that Poland was usually the defendant in these procedures; and this, in turn, alienated much of the public sympathy that had existed in Poland for the League of Nations.

After the international recognition of her eastern frontiers by the Conference of Ambassadors,[23] Poland's position in the League of Nations improved considerably. Problems concerning Danzig and complaints by the German minorities continued to burden the agenda of the League, but they were of smaller moment, and the community of interest between Poland and nations with similar international minority obligations alleviated the political pressure. Although Poland failed to win a seat in the Council in the early 1920's, the participation of her delegates in the works of the League of Nations became more evident. The skillful and broad-minded policy of Foreign Minister Count Alexander Skrzynski[24] enabled the Polish Government to take an active part in the international policy of cooperation and appeasement that characterized this period.

Skrzynski's concept of foreign policy was based on the conviction that Poland should not be a cause of tension in Europe, but
that she should promote a general *détente* and contribute to the
establishment of a lasting peace by conciliation with her neighbors
and friendly cooperation with other nations.[25] His efforts were
fruitful. He straightened out Poland's relations with Czechoslovakia, whose Foreign Minister, Eduard Benes, was received with
great courtesy at Warsaw in April, 1925. During this visit—reciprocated a year later by Skrzynski in Prague—a Treaty of Arbitration and Conciliation, a Commercial Agreement, and an important Liquidation Agreement were signed. In February, 1925, Poland concluded a Concordat with the Holy See, which adjusted
the limits of the dioceses to the actual territory of the reborn republic; it also guaranteed the Catholic Church free exercise of its
spiritual mission and of its administration according to Canon
Law, and re-established the Polish Government's traditional privileges in appointments of the hierarchy. In September, 1925, economic talks with Germany were resumed. Relations with the
Soviet Union also improved. Chicherin found a friendly reception
in Warsaw when he spent a few days there during a journey west.
The raising of Polish legations in France, at the Vatican, and in
other capitals to the rank of embassies were signs of Poland's growing prestige in international affairs.

In a speaking tour of the United States in 1925, Skrzynski approached specifically Polish problems by way of a general evaluation of European politics, assuming the role of spokesman for Europe as a whole.[26] He used the same approach in Geneva during
the debates concerning the Protocol of 1924, which he supported
enthusiastically, confident that it would improve the security of
Europe. When it became known, after the defeat of the Geneva
Protocol, that negotiations had been initiated between France and
England and also between France and Germany, Skrzynski
opened discussions with the Allied powers in order to participate
in the talks. With France, he invoked the argument that a Western pact without the participation of Poland would weaken the
Franco–Polish alliance. With England, he stressed the point that
any such pact ignoring Polish interests could open the way to a

conflict in Eastern Europe. His efforts met with success. Arriving in Locarno after the various delegations were already assembled, he was asked to take part in the deliberations and also in the drafting of documents concerning Poland.[27] He was unable, however, to secure, within the system of the Locarno Treaties, an extension of territorial guarantees to the eastern border of Germany. Inasmuch as the Rhine frontier was fully guaranteed, Poland and Czechoslovakia obtained only partial satisfaction in the form of arbitration and conciliation treaties with Germany and a strengthening of their ties with France.

In Poland itself, Skrzynski found little approval of his policy. When the Locarno Treaties came up for ratification by the Seym, he met strong opposition, especially from right-wing National Democrats, who argued that the treaties would not improve Poland's security but would give Germany the advantage of a permanent seat in the Council of the League of Nations. A motion was presented to postpone ratification until a permanent seat should be granted to Poland. Eventually, a milder resolution was passed and the ratification approved on March 2, 1926.

In the eyes of Poland, her admission to the Council was an absolute necessity because of the German Government's clearly expressed intention to exploit its own position in the League in connection with Danzig and the German minorities.[28] Skrzynski was convinced that Poland would be admitted to the Council on an equal basis with Germany; he had a promise from Chamberlain, the French press favored Poland's claim, and Mussolini strongly backed it.[29] The German Government, however, opposed any further change in the structure of the Council beyond securing a permanent seat for itself and regarded the simultaneous admission of another country—especially Poland—as contrary to the promises given to Stresemann.

After stormy discussions and protracted delays, a compromise solution of this complex problem was arrived at during the September, 1926, session of the Assembly. Germany obtained a permanent seat in the Council, and Poland—whose conciliatory attitude was highly praised—gained re-election rights and joined the Council in a semipermanent status.

Skrzynski had no opportunity to develop further the foreign policy for which he had laid the foundations so carefully and with such understanding. He resigned on May 5, 1926, when the cabinet he had headed since November, 1925, lost the broad parliamentary basis required to stabilize the political and financial situation of the state. Pilsudski's *coup d'état* occurred a week later. When order and legality were re-established, another professional diplomat, August Zaleski, became head of the Ministry of Foreign Affairs.

III

The Quest for Stability: 1926–32

MARSHAL PILSUDSKI's *coup d'état* was primarily motivated by Poland's internal political and financial crisis, which in his opinion necessitated drastic changes in the interplay of parliamentary forces and a broadening of executive power. Yet it seems obvious that international politics also impelled him. Two factors impaired Poland's international position. One was the treaty of guarantee with France, signed within the Locarno system, which weakened the Franco-Polish alliance of 1921 by subordinating automatic mutual assistance to League of Nations procedure. The other was the renewal and amendment, on April 24, 1926, of the Soviet-German Rapallo agreement of 1922, which indicated closer collaboration between two neighbors whose *rapprochement* always implied danger for Poland. However, Pilsudski, gifted with rare political foresight, did not expect within the next five years any major international upheaval involving Poland;[1] he wanted to use this respite to consolidate the country's domestic and international positions.

As soon as peace and order were re-established, the National Assembly, composed of the Seym and the Senate, elected Ignacy Moscicki President of the Republic,[2] the Seym voted constitutional amendments increasing executive power, the problem of the high command of the army was settled by decree, Pilsudski becoming its virtual chief,[3] and, finally, important economic and fiscal reforms were made on the advice of an American financial expert, Professor E. Kemmerer. All these initial steps leading to domestic consolidation were followed by political moves to influence world opinion in favor of the new regime. Marshal Pilsudski, in an interview by Sauerwein, the French journalist, defined his concept of foreign policy by saying, *"nous ne désirons rien . . . nous voulons vivre et nous fortifier dans la paix."*[4]

57

Zaleski's appointment, first as acting Foreign Minister and, after October, 1926, as Minister of Foreign Affairs, was fully consistent with this principle. The new head of the foreign service possessed all the required qualities; also, he enjoyed the confidence of Marshal Pilsudski, who, after May, 1926, was more active in formulating foreign policy than while Chief of State.[5] It was most fortunate that Zaleski was highly popular in French governmental circles, as is evidenced in the complimentary description of his personality in Ambassador Jules Laroche's memoirs.[6] Relations with France, especially military cooperation, were held to be of primary importance, and the Franco-Polish alliance was regarded as the foundation of Poland's international position. Since 1920, a French military mission of highly qualified officers had organized and managed, to the satisfaction of the Polish government, the network of service schools and had supervised the training of the Polish Army. When Marshal Foch visited Poland in May, 1923,[7] a common plan of action in the event of German aggression was worked out, known as the Foch Plan. Despite some differences of opinion on tactical matters, it was continued for a number of years. The treaty of alliance with France had been in force, along with commercial agreements and the military convention, since May, 1922.[8]

After the electoral victory of the Cartel des Gauches in 1924, there were tendencies to narrow the interpretation of the alliance, especially regarding France's guarantee to aid Poland in the event of Soviet aggression. The economic recovery of Germany, in consequence of the acceptance of the Dawes Commission report, as well as the negotiations initiated in February, 1925, by Briand, Chamberlain, and Stresemann, had brought about a new situation in Europe. As a result, the Polish Government was fearful that Germany's revisionism, confronted with the French and English desire for safety on the Rhine, would lead to a compromise at the cost of Poland. Polish political and military leaders attempted to counteract those negative tendencies in Paris and London.[9] But, despite their efforts, the Franco-Polish alliance was subjected to complicated legal interpretation. Doubts were expressed in Paris as to whether France and Poland had the right to grant each other immediate military assistance and not wait for a decision by the League of Nations.

The French Government several times arranged talks in order to adapt the alliance of 1921 to the Locarno agreements. It was clearly not in Poland's interest to clarify controversial points so as to limit mutual obligations.[10] Marshal Pilsudski and, on his advice, Polish military and diplomatic representatives carefully avoided committing Poland to a definite interpretation that would weaken the alliance.

These circumstances did not produce any substantial or tangible change in the relations between the two nations. However, an undercurrent of dissent between Warsaw and Paris became evident after the advent of Pilsudski's regime. Paradoxically, this Polish Government tactic to maintain the full value of the alliance with France brought down on it French accusations of failure to cooperate.

The leaders of the National Democratic Party of Poland, which opposed Pilsudski, contributed to this peculiar state of affairs. For a long time, they had maintained close relations with France, particularly with the French press, and they attempted, with some success, to monopolize Franco-Polish relations for themselves. Because of their constant and sharp opposition to Pilsudski, Poland's domestic frictions interfered with political relations between France and Poland.

On the other hand, the Polish ruling group resented the patronizing attitude of the French and was particularly sensitive to the frequent criticism of Pilsudski and his regime by the French press.

Poland's internal financial problems had an unfortunate effect on French investments there and this created adverse political repercussions. Of several cases, the most conspicuous was that of Zyrardow, a textile mill founded by Frenchmen when Russia ruled Poland. The Polish authorities took harsh measures against its management that were not warranted by Polish fiscal and social policy, and these acts were strongly attacked in the French press and led to frequent diplomatic interventions by France on behalf of the investors. The result was mutual ill-feeling and distrust.

There were still other serious reasons for misunderstanding between the two countries. Poland was apprehensive about France's tendency to pursue her own security without regard for the resulting eastward momentum of German revisionism. Perhaps an even more important cause was the role of the Soviet Union in France's plans for an eastern defense system, but the full import of this factor in Franco-Polish relations emerged clearly only in 1934, in the light of the Eastern Locarno project.

On the other hand, the French Government was annoyed by the steady stream of protests over Danzig and Poland's German minorities that were brought before the League of Nations. The irritation was the greater because of the growing cooperation between Briand and Stresemann. Although the French delegate usually supported the Poles, he felt burdened by the many petty but time-consuming cases. Poland's situation improved considerably the moment she won election to the Council of the League of Nations. Council membership was an advantage for any country, but particularly so for Poland, which had to be prepared for an intensification of various German initiatives.[11] It admitted the Polish delegate to the inner circle of top European statesmen; previously his attendance at the Council table had been merely *ad hoc* and by special invitation.[12]

Aware of this advantage, Zaleski did not spare his efforts, first to obtain a semipermanent seat in the Council for Poland and then to utilize the Geneva forum to build up Poland's prestige in international affairs. His great merit was that in difficult situations he never departed from a statesmanlike and moderate attitude. In the debates of the League of Nations organs, he provided a welcome factor of judgment and sense of proportion. Marshal Pilsudski was skeptical about the efficacy of the League's procedures and authority. His attitude was not changed by his visit to Geneva, in December, 1927, to join in the Council's discussion of Polish-Lithuanian problems. Proof of this is that five years later he expressed doubts about the desirability of Poland's soliciting another re-election to the Council.[13]

Pilsudski's appearance before the Council in 1927 was the result of the importance he attached to relations with Lithuania, which had seriously deteriorated in the preceding two months. The Lithuanian Government, headed by Valdemaras, had complained to the League that it was threatened by war. Pilsudski had no intention whatsoever of attacking Lithuania; moreover, he was anxious to remove obstacles to normal relations between the two nations. Leaving procedural matters to Zaleski, he asked the Lithuanian delegate in a down-to-earth manner whether war or peace existed between the two countries. Valdemaras had no choice but to declare that a state of war no longer existed between Poland and Lithuania. The Council's resolution registered this statement and recommended direct negotiations on the questions in dispute.

After long preliminary talks, the recommended negotiations were inaugurated on March 30, 1928, in Königsberg. But neither these talks nor another series of conversations that took place in June produced any result except for minor improvements in the transport of goods. No diplomatic or consular relations were established between the two countries, and their common borders remained closed.

It has sometimes been said that the Polish Government should have exploited the favorable circumstances of the December, 1927, Council meeting to force an immediate exchange of diplomatic representations. Considering the "unequaled obstinacy"[14] of the Lithuanians, it is doubtful whether such an attempt would have succeeded.

Polish participation in League of Nations activities was of course not limited to specific problems of her relations with neighboring states. The Polish delegation submitted to the 1927 Assembly a draft treaty prohibiting the use of force and recommending peaceful means for settling disputes. The draft was passed unanimously by the Assembly, although only as a resolution. It may rightly be considered a forerunner of the Kellogg-Briand Pact, negotiated and signed a year later by the majority of states.[15]

The most important question that Zaleski had to deal with in Geneva, as well as in direct negotiations with Berlin, was Poland's relations with Germany. Commercial negotiations were fruitless, because Poland was unwilling to grant the German Government's demand for the right of settlement for German citizens. When, moreover, Silesian authorities expelled four directors of German enterprises, the German Government retaliated, and a complete deadlock resulted. Under these circumstances, it was decided to resume personal contact between the two ministers of foreign affairs, Stresemann and Zaleski, in Geneva. They agreed on a new series of negotiations, this time on the diplomatic level. There followed a number of meetings between Rauscher, the German Minister Plenipotentiary to Warsaw, and Lipski, then chief of the Western Department of the Polish Ministry of Foreign Affairs. At these sessions, the most difficult problems were settled, and delegates were appointed to continue with economic negotiations. These delegates concluded several other agreements, the most important being the liquidation convention, which was integrated into the final Hague agreement on the settlement of all war debts.

This step forward in Polish-German relations was the result of pressure exerted on Stresemann by German heavy industry, which regarded Poland as a good market. The success of the negotiations was largely due to Lipski's skill as a negotiator and to Rauscher's personality. He was not the usual German diplomat, recruited from a conservative Prussian background and violently opposed to friendly relations with Poland. He was a native of Württemberg and a former journalist, and instead of seeking a revision of boundaries with Poland, he dismissed this as impossible and felt that more could be gained by establishing friendly cooperation between the two countries.[16]

On the Polish side, Pilsudski clearly desired a *détente*. His general idea was that during the next few years Poland should consolidate her position, and a normal exchange of goods between Poland and Germany would add to Poland's economic stability.

But, in spite of substantial progress in economic relations, a complete return to normal trade was rendered difficult at this time. President von Hindenburg at first refused to ratify the liquidation agreement, thus postponing a commercial treaty that had meanwhile been negotiated. The liquidation agreement was finally ratified a few days later and the treaty was signed, but it never went into effect, because of a change of government in Germany. Until 1934, economic relations with Germany operated on a day-to-day basis, with only partial and provisional agreements.

Stresemann's policy of cooperation with the West had decreased tension in that direction. But it lent force to a growing revisionism directed particularly against Poland. One manifestation of this was support by the German delegation to the League of a large number of petitions and claims submitted by Poland's German minority. In the Council meeting at Lugano in December, 1928, the charges against Polish authorities in Silesia led to a heated discussion. Zaleski stated the Polish view on German-minority activity, whereupon Stresemann lost his composure[17] and announced that he would demand a complete revision of League procedures for protection of minorities. Although Briand, President of the Council, and the British representative expressed disapproval of Zaleski's unexpected intervention, most Council members felt that his courageous denunciation of the agitation by German minorities had exposed the abuse of the system intended to protect minorities. In the final analysis, the exaggerated claims of the German minority groups, together with Stresemann's violent response, served to lessen the pressure exerted on Poland by the German Government. The minority petitions decreased in number, and apparently even Stresemann saw that his tactics were leading nowhere.[18]

The growing influence of nationalistic groups within Germany and the Western powers' tendency to give in to the German desire to rearm gave Pilsudski cause for alarm. The Allied withdrawal from the Rhineland in 1930 weakened France's security and consequently rendered Poland's defense position more difficult. Fearing further concessions by England and France, Pilsudski decided to use the Danzig situation to warn Germany and the West that Poland would, if necessary, defend her interests by force. On July 14, 1932, the destroyer "Wicher" entered the port of Danzig, ostensibly to render customary honors to three small units of the British Navy. However, the destroyer's commander had orders to react forcibly to any insult to his colors. The rights of the Polish Navy in the port of Danzig were unspecified and were at that moment under discussion in the League of Nations.[19] The Danzig Senate strongly protested the presence of the Polish destroyer, but the legal question was by no means clear. The maneuver aroused great indignation in the Council of the League, which was then in session. The representatives of France and England exerted strong pressure on Zaleski for withdrawal of the "Wicher." The incident was closed when the Polish Government declared that it did not intend to attack Danzig. The final result was a definite agreement between Poland and Danzig providing priority for the Polish navy in the port. A subsequent possible incident was averted when a German flotilla entered the port of Danzig and the League asked Poland to avoid a similar show of power at that time.

In conducting Polish relations with the Soviet Union, Zaleski also had to deal with some difficult problems. His predecessor, Skrzynski, had made all-out efforts to create a better atmosphere between the two countries. At that time, the U.S.S.R. strongly opposed conclusion of the Locarno treaties. Chicherin's tactics were to play the card of Poland in his talks with Germany, and at the same time to propose a nonaggression pact to Poland (Poland in her reply suggested including Rumania and the Baltic states in any such agreement). Germany assured Moscow that the Reich's participation in the Locarno system, which would entail membership in the Council of the League, would be of no disadvantage to the Soviets, since Germany could then block any anti-Russian move by the Western powers. In April, 1926, the German and Russian governments renewed and amplified the Rapallo agreement. Thus, German-Soviet collaboration continued to be a potential threat to Poland.

Pilsudski's *coup d'état* in 1926 provoked considerable anxiety in Moscow. At the outset, the Polish Communist Party was favorable, but very shortly it was ordered to create an opposition movement. The Russians suspected that the *coup* had been inspired by England as a first step in Western intervention against Communism.[20] Moscow's distrust of the new Polish Government was reinforced by the belief that the new Foreign Minister, Zaleski, had held anti-Russian feelings during World War I.

Russian misgivings notwithstanding, Pilsudski was inclined to promote collaboration and friendly relations with all neighboring countries. Proof of this was the appointment of Stanislas Patek as Envoy to Moscow.[21] A lawyer before the war, Patek had defended in Czarist courts several Russian revolutionaries who were later to play a role in the Soviet Government, and he was therefore well received in Moscow.

Amid the mutual tendencies to improve relations, the Soviet Envoy to Warsaw, Voikov, was assassinated by a young Russian *émigré*. Moscow again saw evidence of a conspiracy by the West, and there were even signs of military preparations in Russia. The Polish Government did everything it could to calm Soviet fears, and in this effort Patek proved extremely valuable.

In December, 1928, Litvinov, Soviet Commissar of Foreign Affairs, proposed that the Kellogg-Briand Pact be put into force immediately by Poland, the U.S.S.R., and Lithuania. Poland again requested inclusion of Rumania and the Baltic states. The "Litvinov Protocol" was signed in Moscow in February, 1929, by Estonia, Latvia, Poland, Rumania, and the U.S.S.R., and, somewhat later, Lithuania.

In 1930, internal difficulties in the Soviet Union, the threat of Japanese expansion in the Far East, and the conciliatory attitude toward Germany shown by England and France combined to induce the Soviet Government to seek further *rapprochement* with Warsaw. Negotiations for a nonaggression treaty were intensified, and, in July, 1932, a pact was finally signed in Moscow.

These measures manifested the U.S.S.R. Government's eagerness to play a prominent part in the Disarmament Conference to be held in Geneva in February, 1932. The Soviet Union was in an exceptional position: She was a member of the conference but not bound by the Covenant of the League, to which she did not belong. Germany was expected to put forward its revisionist aims and to demand equality of armaments with the great powers—in a word, cancellation of the Versailles disarmament clauses. Pilsudski feared that France, backed by England, would yield to German pressure. Under these circumstances, the Polish delegation's tactics were limited to promotion of moral disarmament, which should precede technical arms limitation, and of a very simple, technical plan for arms limitation.

Discussion at the conference soon revealed two opposing camps: One advanced the principle of security and was represented mainly by France; the other stressed the principle of equality of armaments and was argued mainly by Germany. Germany clearly had in mind a revision of the military clauses of the Treaty of Versailles, and the resulting possibility of massive rearmament that could lead to territorial revision.

Pilsudski's apprehensions proved accurate when, in December, 1932, the great powers, together with Germany, accepted the Geneva declaration on German armament equality.[22] In Poland, this was interpreted as a surrender by France that considerably weakened her as an ally. Before the conference was resumed in 1933, Hitler had come to power and the world situation had changed completely. In October, Germany withdrew from the conference and so brought about its collapse.

One further matter belongs to the last period of Zaleski's tenure: the attempt to organize a Central European agrarian bloc. At the Geneva economic conference in 1930, the agricultural countries of Central and Southeastern Europe developed a spontaneous spirit of cooperation. As a result, the Polish Government invited Bulgaria, Czechoslovakia, Estonia, Hungary, Latvia, Lithuania, Rumania, and Yugoslavia to send delegations to Warsaw in June, 1930, for a conference to improve the bargaining position of the agricultural countries in relation to that of the highly industrialized states of Western Europe. All except Lithuania were represented. A permanent organization was created, and it was decided that economic experts would meet annually to determine common policy for the bloc; a general conference would convene from time to time. During the next few years the bloc achieved a fair amount of cooperation and was beneficial to the economic life of its members. But under the impact of the political changes of the thirties, solidarity declined among the Central and Eastern European agrarian countries. This led to the deterioration and eventual dissolution of the agrarian bloc.

In November, 1932, on his return from Geneva, Zaleski submitted his resignation. His withdrawal, it is generally held, was due to the difficult position he had found himself in during the Council session on the "Wicher" incident.

During his relatively long tenure—from May, 1926, to December, 1932—Zaleski had represented Poland in most of the important international events and discussions. His ability and unfailing tact and courtesy had won him considerable esteem in international circles, and he had rendered great services to his country. Unswerving in promoting political stability based on permanent international obligations, he advocated ideas then prevailing among statesmen of the Western powers and often voiced in the League of Nations. His wise and persevering service to the cause of peace increased world confidence in the steady development of Poland and in the moderation of her foreign policy.

As Pilsudski's five-year period of consolidation drew to a close, some changes occurred in his manner of dealing with domestic and international problems. The authority of the executive was reinforced, and the struggle between Pilsudski and the Parliament at times became intense. In 1930, the Seym was dissolved and new elections were announced. Soon afterward, the main leaders of a congress of opposition parties held in Kraków were arrested, accused of activities against the state, and incarcerated in the military prison in Brzesc on the Bug (Brest Litovsk). Reports soon circulated about brutalities inflicted on the prisoners. In spite of the indignation that this aroused in the press and in public opinion, the Nonpartisan Bloc of Cooperation with the Government won a majority in the elections.

Pilsudski won his struggle with Parliament, but at the cost of detrimental effects abroad. Events gave some color of truth to unfriendly charges that the Pilsudski regime was a strong-man dictatorship, and these charges were not without effect on foreign opinion. This impression was strengthened by incidents in eastern Galicia. After Pilsudski came to power, he developed a program to satisfy the aspirations of the Ukrainian population in Poland.[23] But during the first few years no minister of the interior acted on it. The result was an increasing dissatisfaction among the Ukrainians, stirred up by Ukrainian groups in Berlin, Moscow, and

Prague. Tension was greatest in 1930, when terrorism was resorted to by secret Ukrainian organizations. Their campaign of sabotage provoked drastic countermeasures by the government, allegedly to protect the local populace and its property. The Ukrainian leaders protested to the League of Nations against the behavior of the police and armed forces.[24] In January, 1932, the League concluded that "Poland was not carrying on a repressive . . . policy" against the Ukrainians, but that individual officials had committed excesses and had been duly punished.[25] In the end, the Polish Government adopted a more conciliatory attitude and announced that it would seek a better approach to the problem of the Ukrainians in Poland.

The selection of Colonel Józef Beck as Undersecretary of State, on December 6, 1930, was a sign that a change was forthcoming in foreign policy, too.[26] His appointment indicated greater activity in international affairs. Beck, during his two years as second in command, gradually increased his control over political activities and the technical problems of the Polish foreign service. He dealt particularly with questions of the Baltic region, Danzig, and the Soviet Union, and Zaleski gave him a free hand in these areas. It was generally believed that Pilsudski intended him to succeed Zaleski. So it was not surprising that, upon the latter's resignation in 1932, Beck was appointed Minister of Foreign Affairs.

IV

Efforts to Reinforce Security: 1932–35

WHEN BECK TOOK OVER the Ministry of Foreign Affairs, diplomatic relations with the Soviet Union had achieved a degree of calm. But relations with Germany were uneasy. Long and difficult negotiations had eliminated most of the nonpolitical problems in a manner that could be considered favorable for Poland.[1] But German revisionist propaganda continued with even greater impetus after 1930, when former Minister for the Occupied Territories Treviranus delivered a series of impassioned speeches on the subject, and reached its peak with the interview Hitler gave the British journalist Colonel Etherton.

An interesting interpretation of this, based on the documents of the Nuremberg trials, is given by Lipski.[2] His theory is that this constant and costly effort to persuade Germany and the world that the Corridor had to disappear was connected with a plan for a limited war. As soon as world opinion was sufficiently persuaded of the necessity of recognizing German claims, a brief military action was to occupy the territory, thus cutting off Poland's access to the sea. Lipski compares this *Verstärkungsplan* with the later German assault on Czechoslovakia.

The revisionist drive may also have been provoked by other circumstances. The consequences of the German economic crisis of the 1930's made the government want to distract the people from domestic problems, and the catchword *Saisonstaat* suggested Poland as the easiest object of aggression. It is necessary to keep in mind that the Germans had interpreted the Wilsonian principles to mean that Germany should retain all the territories in her possession before World War I.[3] Hence their grievances about the Versailles treaty.

German military circles warned against premature and dangerous measures that could ignite a preventive war. They undertook studies of an enlarged plan that considered the possibility of a war on two fronts. Hitler, on coming to power, took into account this opinion and looked for the opportunity to build up Germany's military power. As usual, Pilsudski diagnosed these trends, and concluded that it was time to get Hitler's reaction to a test of strength.

On March 6, 1933, it was made known that a Polish Navy transport, the "Wilja," had landed about 100 soldiers in Westerplatte, a Polish munitions depot on the border of Danzig's harbor. According to previous agreements, the garrison of Westerplatte was to number 88 officers and men. In justification of the increase to almost 200 men, Poland quoted rumors that the Nazis might launch an attack on the depot, an attack that would be facilitated by the recent replacement of the port police by local Danzig policemen.[4] The High Commissioner of the League of Nations, on receiving a complaint by the Danzig Senate, stated that an *action directe* had occurred, and referred the matter to the Council of the League. The Polish Government filed a similar complaint, protesting against the disbanding of the port police without previous consultation. The Western powers reacted with unusual alarm and criticism of Poland. Germany, not feeling ready to take up the challenge, exerted influence on Danzig authorities to limit the conflict. The problem was finally solved in Geneva by compromise: The Polish Government agreed to withdraw their additional soldiers on condition that the port police be restored.

If Pilsudski's objective had been, as it seemed, to test Hitler's reaction, he had to conclude that the Reich was not yet willing to go to war—and also that the Western powers would not cooperate in an action against Hitlerism. He therefore decided to use diplomatic channels in an attempt to reach a direct understanding with Germany.

Immediately after the Westerplatte incident, Poland was faced with the Four-Power Pact. England and France had failed to reach a compromise with Germany during the Disarmament Conference. But the Western powers were still ready to confer with Germany about disarmament on any occasion. When Ramsay MacDonald and Sir John Simon came to Rome in March, 1933, they showed interest in Mussolini's plan for an agreement by England, France, Italy, and Germany to use their preponderant political and material power to maintain peace and solve existing conflicts. The intention of making territorial revisions was expressed in Article 2 of the draft. Since Mussolini had in the past strongly opposed the idea of the *Anschluss,* it could be inferred that his intention was to shift Germany's territorial ambitions toward Poland.[5] Confidential information received by the Polish Foreign Ministry confirmed this assumption.

An immediate and strong reaction was voiced by Poland and by the Little Entente, the countries most interested in maintaining the territorial *status quo* in Central and East Central Europe. The Polish reaction was by far the most spectacular. The recently appointed Ambassador to Rome, Count George Potocki,[6] resigned, expressing his criticism of the Italian proposal in a letter to the Polish Foreign Minister. Beck prepared to journey to Prague and Belgrade in an attempt to develop a common policy against the proposed pact, and to Paris to persuade the French Government that Poland would never allow a group of other powers to decide matters of immediate interest to her. His memoirs explain that this journey never took place because it was deferred by Pilsudski's illness, and in the meantime Benes had been persuaded to abandon his opposition to the pact.[7]

After a number of changes in the original draft, made at the insistence of France and Great Britain, the pact was rendered harmless—and also useless. It was initialed in Rome on June 5, but never came into force.

Poland's main motives for opposing the Four-Power Pact were (1) fear that France would forsake the interests of her allies when faced by the revisionist tendencies of her partners in the pact, and (2) the conviction that a directorate of great powers should not decide questions that vitally concerned other countries. This episode contributed to Pilsudski's decision not to rely on Western support but to seize any opportunity for direct talks with Germany. At first, Pilsudski intended to send the Undersecretary of State, Count Szembek, to Berlin to confer with Hitler on questions of principle. It was necessary to avoid involving the German Foreign Office, known to be unfriendly toward Poland. But the Polish Minister in Berlin, Wysocki, reported that a meeting with Hitler must be arranged through the Wilhelmstrasse.[8] Moreover, he expressed doubt as to whether Hitler would receive a Polish spokesman, since he was careful not to antagonize his nationalist supporters. After a further exchange of information between the Berlin Legation and Warsaw, it was decided to entrust the mission to Wysocki himself.[9]

The meeting took place on May 2, 1933, in the presence of the Reich's Minister of Foreign Affairs, Baron von Neurath. Wysocki followed his instructions exactly. He limited the subject of his *démarche* to the affirmation that relations between Germany and Poland were most unsatisfactory and that the problems of Danzig were continuously alarming Polish public opinion, which was particularly sensitive to all incidents connected with Poland's free access to the sea and the rights Poland had acquired in Danzig. He therefore requested the Chancellor to consider issuing a declaration that Germany had no intention of violating those rights. Hitler's answer was very extensive and involved a broad discussion of the relations between the two countries. At the end of the interview, Wysocki suggested the publication of a communiqué in which Hitler's peaceful intentions would be expressed. The Foreign Office, displeased with Hitler's willingness to declare that the German Government would keep the treaty provisions concerning Poland, tried to substitute a meaningless text. A compromise was reached when Warsaw agreed to answer Hitler's communiqué with a similar one to be published after Beck conferred with the German Minister in Warsaw, von Moltke.

The two communiqués evoked great interest abroad. It was a complete reversal of the situation that had prevailed only a few weeks before. Poland's international position was strengthened. With few exceptions, it was felt that the general atmosphere of European politics had improved with the elimination of the danger of an armed conflict in that area. In some capitals, however, rumors circulated about a secret agreement under which Poland would refrain from opposing German occupation of Austria. In a speech before the Reichstag on May 17, Hitler again declared his peaceful intentions toward Poland and France, and his intent to adhere to the treaties. Thus, the purpose of the Polish Government was attained.

In recognition of his excellent performance of a difficult task, Wysocki was appointed Ambassador to Italy, to succeed Count Potocki, who had resigned. Wysocki was replaced in Berlin by Józef Lipski, for many years director of the Western department and consequently the ranking expert on Polish-German relations. His dexterity in handling delicate political problems, combined with brilliant intelligence and untiring energy, singled him out as one of the most talented diplomats of his generation.

Lipski presented his credentials to President von Hindenburg on October 18. Several weeks later, on November 15, he was received by Hitler in the presence of Foreign Minister Baron von Neurath. In this interview Lipski, on Pilsudski's instructions, stated that Germany's withdrawal from the League of Nations had deprived Poland of the Covenant's guarantee, an element of her security, and raised the question whether this loss could not be compensated by some bilateral arrangement. In his answer Hitler repeated his former assurances of peaceful intentions toward Poland and proposed a treaty excluding war between the two nations.[10] A few days later, a tentative draft of a declaration proclaiming this principle was submitted to Pilsudski by von Moltke. Both sides considered the matter strictly confidential; the only information made public was an official German press communiqué stating that both governments had resolved "to renounce all application of force in their reciprocal relations, with a view to strengthening European peace."[11]

Pilsudski had carefully calculated all political factors. The most important one to be taken into consideration was the reaction of France to the new Polish-German relationship. When Beck became Foreign Minister, he faced several problems that interfered with the smooth working of the Polish alliance with France. First, there was the discrepancy between the stipulations of the alliance and the guarantee treaty of Locarno. Pilsudski had avoided discussing the subject with France, and thus both agreements remained in force. The Polish Government felt that the evacuation of the Rhineland had weakened France's ability to fulfill her treaty obligations. Nonetheless, Pilsudski still considered the alliance with France essential. He had a very high opinion of the French Army, although he doubted whether the French political leaders would use it to block German ambitions.

The appointment of Beck did not help Franco-Polish relations, as the French had little confidence in him. In addition, he had to deal from the very start with matters in which the two governments were not in agreement, such as the Four-Power Pact and the French plan submitted at the Disarmament Conference. In spite of this, his official relations with the Quai d'Orsay (Foreign Ministry) were correct, at times even cordial. He had paid an official visit to Paris in September, 1933, and was received by Premier Daladier and Foreign Minister Paul-Boncour with full honors.[12] Yet there remained the essential difference of approach to the German problem. The unannounced negotiation between Poland and Germany created suspicion in Paris that Poland was contemplating a complete reversal of its attitude toward France. This reaction was excessive, for, although the French Government was not notified in advance of Lipski's visit to Hitler on November 15, on the very next day Beck gave a full account of the meeting to the French Ambassador in Warsaw. A few days later, Pilsudski did the same for General d'Arbonneau, the French military attaché, and the presence of the Polish Chief of Staff gave this meeting an official military character.[13] It was apparent that Pilsudski hoped that this conversation would be reported to the French Premier and would evoke a clearer statement of the French position and eliminate the atmosphere of suspicion.

In spite of this, the French Government continued to criticize Poland for not consulting it in advance, although at that time the French tendency also was to reach an understanding with Hitler on disarmament.

After the Hitler-Lipski meeting, Pilsudski warned Beck that the talks with Germany would greatly complicate Polish relations with the Soviet Union. It was necessary to maintain good relations with Moscow, he said, but this would demand patience and perseverance.[14]

When the Soviet-Polish nonaggression treaty was signed in Moscow in July, 1932, the Germans, particularly in military circles, were seriously worried. They feared that, in the event of a conflict with Poland, they would be unable to obtain military aid from the U.S.S.R. The Soviet Government tried to allay Germany's apprehensions but continued to build up its system of agreements with Poland.[15]

During the Disarmament Conference in Geneva, Litvinov proposed to the Poles an agreement defining aggression. Poland, as in previous instances, demanded that the Baltic states bordering Russia participate in the negotiations. Reluctantly, Moscow agreed. For her part, she invited Iran, Turkey, and Afghanistan. The Conference was held in London, and after laborious discussions the convention was signed on July 3, 1933. During these diplomatic developments, nonofficial contacts were promoted on both sides. A cultural and intellectual exchange took place when the Editor in Chief of *Izvestiya*, Radek and Miedzinski, Editor in Chief of *Gazeta Polska*, exchanged visits and had a number of semiofficial interviews.[16] These circumstances reduced Soviet suspicion and left Poland free to continue talks with Germany.

In December, the Soviet Government proposed to Poland that they jointly guarantee the independence of the Baltic states. The text submitted by the Russians could be so interpreted that any change in the political, military, or economic structure of those countries might serve as an excuse for intervention by the guarantors. Strictest secrecy was requested. The Polish Government did not refuse outright, but again demanded that the Baltic governments participate in the negotiations. However, the Baltic states were unwilling to accept such a guarantee, and the proposal was abandoned.[17] To offset any negative impression created by her uncooperativeness in this matter, Poland suggested that Minister Beck visit Moscow. The Soviet Government hastily proffered an official invitation.

Meanwhile, negotiations on the Polish-German nonaggression declaration were reaching the last stage. A draft submitted to Pilsudski by von Moltke on November 27 was considered unsatisfactory from the Polish viewpoint on several counts. The main

objection was that it contained the obligation to submit to conciliation or arbitration *all* controversies between Poland and Germany,
and this could be interpreted as including territorial questions.
Such an obligation would weaken the guarantees contained in the
Covenant of the League of Nations and in Poland's alliance
treaties. The draft had to be analyzed, revised, and renegotiated.[18]
But no further action was taken in December. Pilsudski had left
for Vilna, and it was obvious that he intended to delay the final
stage of the negotiations. After Christmas, however, when he
learned that France had resumed disarmament talks with Germany, Pilsudski returned to the problem of the Polish-German
declaration, fearing that French tactics would render Poland's
position more difficult. Polish observations were formulated and a
counterdraft was delivered to Baron von Neurath on January 9,
1934. After some deliberations by legal experts, a formula cover-
ing previous international obligations and acceptable to both
parties was arrived at, and the final text was agreed upon. Lipski
and Baron von Neurath signed it for their governments on January
26, 1934.[19]

The gist of the declaration was that the signatories renounced
recourse to force in settling their disputes. They would base their
relations on the principles of the Pact of Paris—the Kellogg-Briand
Pact. All existing international obligations of both parties were declared to be unaffected, and domestic questions were excluded.
Disputes were to be solved by peaceful means. The declaration
was concluded for ten years, and after this period could be renounced upon six months' notice.

While the last discussions were under way in Berlin, Beck was
in Geneva, where he presided over the League of Nations Council.
Since Paul-Boncour, the French Foreign Minister, was there, too,
Beck informed him of the negotiations with Germany, but he
withheld specific details and did not mention the date of the
signing, which actually was not yet established. Beck inquired
when Ambassador Laroche, then in Paris, would be back in Poland, for he intended to give him important information on his
return to Warsaw.[20]

When news of the signing of the declaration reached Paris, French Government circles were indignant and deeply resentful not to have been consulted, or at least informed, in advance. Officially, an attitude of approval was adopted, but the resentment of the Quai d'Orsay long persisted, although the Polish Government gave all possible assurances that its attitude toward France had not changed. Pilsudski received Ambassador Laroche in the presence of Minister Beck and acquainted him personally with all the details of the negotiations. He assured him that Poland had given Germany no commitments other than those stated in the declaration. He emphasized that Poland had retained full freedom of action and that, if France would initiate an active policy toward Germany, she could count on full cooperation from Poland. Pilsudski's explanations to the French and Rumanian ambassadors were intended to provide the allied governments with full and frank information on Poland's action and her intentions toward Germany.[21] They clarified the situation and should have eliminated any suspicions of additional, secret commitments by Poland.[22] In his conversation with Laroche Pilsudski also denied that Poland had committed herself on the Austrian question—and so gave the lie to a rumor circulated in connection with the events in Vienna and the assassination of Chancellor Dolfuss.

As an aftermath of the German-Polish agreement, the diplomatic representatives of both countries were raised to the rank of ambassador in October.

Pilsudski's warning that great effort would be required to smooth relations with the Soviet Union after conclusion of the nonaggression declaration with Germany made it clear that Beck must take rapid and decisive action. He had been officially invited to visit Moscow, the pretext being that he would return the visit that Chicherin had paid to Poland in 1925. Actually, Beck's main objective was to convince the Soviet Government that Poland had not committed herself to Germany. The timing of his journey— after the signing of the Polish-German declaration but before its ratification—demonstrated Polish intention to reassure Moscow on this point. In his memoirs, Beck relates the general instructions given him by Pilsudski: He was to create an amicable atmosphere but maintain a constant guard against being drawn into the dangerous path of political collaboration with the U.S.S.R.[23]

The visit took place in mid-February. The receptions were attended by the most important leaders of Soviet society, except military figures who had been prominent in the 1920 Soviet-Polish war. Stalin, who at that time held no government office, was not present at the official reception given by Litvinov, the People's Commissar of Foreign Affairs, and Beck did not ask to be received by him. On a visit to the City Council, Beck was greeted with apparent spontaneity. A gala performance at the opera gave him and his party an opportunity to assess the friendly and cordial reaction of the public to their Polish guests. At the conclusion of his visit, the official communiqué stressed the *rapprochement* that had been achieved and announced that both governments had decided to raise their legations to the rank of embassy.

Beck returned to Warsaw in time to proceed to the ratification of the German-Polish nonaggression declaration. Poland had attained an almost perfect balance of security agreements with her two powerful neighbors.

The change in relations between Poland and Germany had an immediate effect on Danzig's attitude toward Poland, the barometer of Polish-German relations. In May, 1933, elections for the Danzig Assembly (*Volkstag*) gave the National Socialist Party 50 per cent of the seats, a greater percentage than it commanded in Germany itself, and Rauschning, a member of the Nazi party and a former leader of the German minority in Poland, became President of the Senate. This produced a complete reversal in the attitude of the Danzig administration. Rauschning and the Senate Vice-President, Greiser, also a Nazi, revived the custom of paying an official visit to the Polish Government. They were received in Warsaw in July, 1933, with courtesy and attention. It became clear that the new Danzig administration, acting in line with Berlin's policy, was endeavoring to improve relations with Poland and to settle all pending problems by direct negotiation with Warsaw. Several important agreements were concluded about Polish use of the port of Danzig and the rights of Polish citizens in Danzig. During their stay in Warsaw, the Danzig officials were received by Pilsudski, and a few months later, the Polish Prime Minister[24] returned the visit.

Rauschning, a man of great intellect and a German nationalist, envisioned Danzig as a link between Germany and Poland. For a short time, he was able to interest Hitler in his concept of a firm and stable German policy of collaboration with Poland. At Hitler's request, he approached Pilsudski to suggest a meeting between him and the Fuehrer. Pilsudski, however, was disinclined to meet the German dictator, whose ruthless drive to power and limitless ambitions he judged severely.[25]

In 1934, the happy state of affairs in Danzig came to an end. Rauschning became involved in a conflict with the leader of the Nazi Party in Danzig, a man named Forster, and when Hitler took the side of the latter, Rauschning resigned his office. Greiser, who succeeded him, was a man of different caliber; he obediently carried out the orders from Hitler and the Nazi Party and had no desire to improve relations with Poland in the interest of Danzig.[26] His aim was to integrate Danzig into the German social and economic framework as rapidly as possible. Inevitably, this provoked new difficulties and conflicts with Poland and the League of Nations.

The German-Polish nonaggression declaration had introduced an element of agreement and cooperation into Polish-Danzig relations. But this did not relieve the ruthless pressure applied in Danzig's domestic affairs by the Nazi Party. At first, however, Greiser continued the policy of his predecessor.

The most important result of Beck's visit to Moscow was the ten-year extension, on May 3, 1934, of the 1932 nonaggression treaty. Now the agreement was to continue until December 31, 1945.[27]

The U.S.S.R. had long avoided participating in world affairs and regarded the League of Nations with scorn and contempt, but now the rise of anti-Communist Nazism in Germany caused a reversal in Soviet foreign policy. The Disarmament Conference supplied a convenient ground for the reappearance of the Soviet Union on the international scene.

The Hugenberg memorandum and the Reichstag fire, with the resultant charges against Communists, as well as the excesses against them and the diatribes of Hitler, produced uneasiness and fear in Moscow, and induced the Soviet Government to seek closer collaboration with nations similarly apprehensive about the resurgence of aggressive German nationalism. Hence, Moscow made conciliatory moves toward Warsaw and Paris.

For France, the desire to resume cooperation with the Soviets was dictated by like feelings. French leaders regarded the failure of the Disarmament Conference and Germany's withdrawal from the League of Nations as threats to peace that necessitated an effort to win Russia's participation in the French system of security in Eastern Europe.

In the fall of 1933, Litvinov, who was considered the exponent of the Politburo's pro-Western camp, approached the French Foreign Minister, Paul-Boncour, suggesting mutual-security arrangements. Conversations were continued between the Quai d'Orsay and the Soviet Embassy in Paris. Louis Barthou, on becoming Foreign Minister of France after the Daladier government fell in February, 1934, decided to force the issue of disarmament with Germany and to organize among the nations east of Germany—the principal one being the Soviet Union—a working system of consultation and mutual assistance. His first step was to accept an invitation from the Polish Government to visit Warsaw. (His predecessor, Paul-Boncour, had announced a few months earlier his intention to return the visit of Beck to Paris, but changes in the French Government had prevented Boncour from coming to Warsaw.) Barthou's principal objective was to appraise the strength of the alliance and to clear up Franco-Polish relations in the wake of the Polish-German nonaggression declaration. Despite repeated and sincere assurances by the Poles, many people in France, even at the Quai d'Orsay, still suspected that Poland had concluded some sinister secret agreement with Germany.[28]

Barthou arrived in Warsaw for a three-day visit on April 22, 1934. In terms of receptions, ceremonies, and public displays of warm feelings toward France and himself, the visit was a great success. His frank and comprehensive talks with Pilsudski and Beck, his conversations with other members of the Polish Government, and his contacts with political circles should have convinced Barthou that Poland still regarded her alliance with France as the cornerstone of her foreign policy and that the agreement with Germany in no way impinged on the alliance. Count Szembek, at that time Undersecretary of State, gives in his *Journal* a very detailed record of Barthou's conversation with Marshal Pilsudski.[29] A fairly complete account of the whole visit appears in the memoirs of French Ambassador Laroche.[30] The cordiality with which Barthou was received and entertained and the sympathy and respect accorded him were so many proofs of France's popularity in Poland.

However, it is undeniable that Poland and France had each experienced a certain amount of disillusionment because of positions taken by the other. French suspicions about the Polish-German agreement were matched by Polish resentment at France's lack of determination in the disarmament question and her intention to draw the Soviet Union into her eastern defense system. Pilsudski could not understand France's lack of reaction to German rearmament, her hesitations and concessions, and, even worse, her criticism of actions taken by Poland to demonstrate that Hitler would yield to a display of force. He believed that these conditions justified him in making a deal with Germany that would, at least temporarily, ease the Polish-German tension, remove the continuous revisionist pressure, and relieve Poland of her difficulties in Danzig —an economic and strategic factor of primary importance. France could rightly complain that the Polish Government had not employed the obligatory consultation procedure and had failed to inform her ally about matters of common interest. A motive, if not an excuse, for Poland's tactics can be found in the hostility and distrust the French directed at Beck. It was one more factor working gradually to weaken the links between the two allies.

History, "whose mills grind slowly," will reach a more accurate judgment. Now evidence for a definitive judgment on the merits and demerits of both sides is still incomplete. Nevertheless, there are in print several memoirs, essays, and collections of documents that prove that the revisionist propaganda, aimed at depriving

Poland of her access to the sea, was efficacious in France.[31] A study of the memoirs of Léon Noël, French Ambassador to Poland, is enlightening, especially where he describes his efforts to limit or suppress France's mutual-assistance obligation to Poland because in the event of German aggression against France, Polish aid would be given anyway.[32]

During his conversation with Pilsudski, Barthou tried to clarify the reciprocal military obligations resulting from the various agreements in force between France and Poland. The most important of these, the military convention of 1921, had never been adapted to the more recent guarantee treaty. Pilsudski agreed to receive a military expert recommended by Barthou. But General Debeney, who came to Warsaw in July, could not persuade Pilsudski to arrive at any adjustment or interpretation of the agreements. It was clear that the Marshal was content to let doubts continue as to the exact meaning of Polish and French reciprocal obligations. He strongly preferred this to a discussion that could water down the clear obligation of immediate mutual assistance, which he had personally negotiated in Paris in 1921. Cooperation between the French and Polish general staffs, at times very close and fruitful, continued in spite of the haziness of the military agreements.

At the time Barthou was in Warsaw discussing the Franco-Polish alliance, he was also preparing the ground for his Eastern Pact plan, and was trying to sound out what Poland's attitude would be. Actual negotiations, however, were started only when all details of the pact had been agreed upon with Litvinov, and adequate preparation had been made for the Soviet Union's election to a permanent seat in the League of Nations Council. Then Barthou instructed Ambassador Laroche to acquaint Beck with the mechanics of the pact. The scheme was complicated. The first part provided for a mutual-assistance pact between the U.S.S.R., the four Baltic states, Poland, Czechoslovakia, and Germany. The second part committed the Soviet Union to assume obligations identical to those of England and Italy in the Locarno Pact and France to participate in the guarantees in the east, subject to League of Nations procedures. Barthou gave additional information to Beck in Geneva on June 4, 1934.[33]

For Poland, the critical factor in the pact was the introduction of preponderant Soviet influence into the East Central and Baltic areas of Europe. This could render the Franco-Polish alliance meaningless, since Russia's geographic position and power would make her dominant in deciding security problems in that area. It was improbable that Germany would accept the invitation to take part in the pact. If Poland joined, she would destroy the equilibrium established by her nonaggression arrangements, depriving herself of her relative freedom of action. The participation of Lithuania and Czechoslovakia, whose territories Poland had no special reason to guarantee, and the nonparticipation of Rumania, Poland's only ally in Eastern Europe, created additional difficulties. Without rejecting Barthou's proposals, Beck explained to him the position of his country and the reasons that compelled the Polish Government to undertake a most careful approach to such an alignment. Finally, in a lengthy memorandum, he summed up the conditions under which Poland could consider joining the pact.[34] But a thorough analysis of the memorandum leads to the conclusion that it was a careful and well-documented refusal to take part.

The most striking weakness of the Eastern Pact was the absence of Great Britain, which gave only lukewarm support to the French undertaking. Thus, the project was devoid of the very factor that was vital to France's position in Europe. The U.S.S.R. would dominate the plan, the more so because Germany, invited to join by Litvinov on his passage through Berlin on June 6, declined to do so.

Since Germany's participation had been from the start a prerequisite for Poland's adherence, the only result of the long negotiation was the conclusion of mutual-security agreements between the Soviet Union and France and between the Soviet Union and Czechoslovakia. Barthou did not live to see even the partial realization of his plan; mortally wounded by the assassin of King Alexander of Yugoslavia, he died in Marseilles on October 9, 1934. His successor, Laval, continued the negotiations. He persuaded the British Government to join France in an initiative whereby the Eastern Pact would be combined with a military agreement and an air-force convention. But when Hitler decreed the rearmament of Germany,[35] it became evident that this broader scheme was doomed. A last effort to realize the second version of the Eastern Pact was undertaken by the British Government. Sir John Simon, Foreign Minister, and Anthony Eden traveled to Berlin, and Eden alone subsequently continued on to Moscow and Warsaw. Their conversations had only one result: They threw additional light on the reasons for the failure of the Eastern Pact.

The U.S.S.R. was the only country to benefit from the treaties that resulted from these protracted, difficult negotiations. The admission to the League of Nations and the mutual assistance treaties with France and Czechoslovakia enabled her to expand Soviet political influence into Western and Central Europe and to play a more active part in world politics.

In spite of the fundamentally different reasons for the German and Polish refusals to join the Eastern Pact, a solidarity of attitude was inferred from them. Unfortunately for Poland, this added weight to the suspicion that she was acting in concert with Germany against her ally, France. In Paris and in Moscow, the alleged "German-Polish community of action" was viewed as confirmation of the opinion that the Polish Government had decided on a reversal of policy, a *tour de valse*. Again, a paradoxical situation had been created by France's efforts to strengthen her security. French public opinion accused Beck of sinister pro-German conspiracies, but it was in fact the divergence of Polish and Russian, and of Polish and Czechoslovakian, interests that forced Poland, against her intentions, to take a stand similar to Germany's.

The admission of the U.S.S.R. to the League of Nations as a permanent member of the Council prompted Beck to undertake two actions that added substance to the criticism of his policy. Mindful of the difficulties that Poland had had to cope with in the League when Germany had exploited minority problems for political advantage, Beck decided to eliminate the possibility of Russian recourse to comparable tactics. After careful preparation and after submitting a formal draft resolution for generalizing minority protection, he declared to the Assembly that the Polish

Government felt "itself compelled to refuse . . . cooperation with international organizations in the matter . . . of minority protection" so long as no general system of minority protection was introduced.[36] The declaration, completely unexpected, aroused considerable protest, because it was taken as a unilateral denunciation of the minority treaty. But analysis of Beck's statement shows that it was a denunciation of the procedure. The protection of minorities, according to the treaties and declarations that had been imposed on a number of nations, provided that only individual members of the Council could introduce motions on this issue. In the course of years, a complicated procedure had been developed for the examination of petitions from minorities. In spite of the principle assigning individual responsibility to a Council member who placed before the Council a minority case, the practice of appointing committees, usually composed of three members, led to the elimination of such responsibility. The minority treaties had been drafted carefully so as to prevent political action against a state through its minorities—but the procedure was not a part of the treaties; it had been gradually introduced and accepted by the states that had subscribed to obligations in minority protection. It could, therefore, undergo changes, or be replaced by another procedure, or even be annulled. The Little Entente powers, which for many years had shared Poland's attitude toward this procedure, refused in 1934 to continue their fight to generalize the protection of minorities, largely because of the personal opinions of Benes and Titulescu.

Despite the strong criticism of Beck's action, no serious opposition to his declaration was voiced. In Poland, public opinion welcomed the denunciation of the procedure regarded as a humiliating limitation of national sovereignty, and Beck was the object of appreciation and gratitude.

There was still another precaution to take against Moscow. The Soviet Union's admission to the League of Nations added a new and complicating factor to her relations with Poland, and the Polish Government considered it necessary to take measures to prevent dilution of existing agreements in the less explicit obligations under the Covenant. With France, the superimposing of the Locarno system had confused the obligation of immediate assistance contained in bilateral agreements. To avoid a similar experience with Russia, the Polish Government suggested to Moscow an exchange of notes stating that the reciprocal relations of the U.S.S.R. and Poland would, after the Soviet Union entered the League, continue to be based on all the agreements existing between them. Beck made acceptance of his proposal a condition for his support of Moscow's admission to the League. The Soviet Government agreed, and Poland supported its bid to enter the League.[37]

Poland's demand, although accepted without difficulties, implied a degree of distrust of the Soviet Union. It therefore contributed to the gradual deterioration of relations between Warsaw and Moscow, which began when Poland voiced doubts about the Eastern Pact, and reached its peak in 1938–39.

During discussions between France and Poland on the Eastern Pact, two countries were repeatedly mentioned—Lithuania and Czechoslovakia. Each occupied a particular position with regard to Poland. As has been related, Lithuania had no diplomatic relations with Poland. Thus Beck, in his talks with Barthou, cited Lithuania as an example of the contradictions inherent in the concept of the Eastern Pact. How could Poland exchange mutual guarantees with a country that obstinately refused to establish normal relations with her?

The problem of Lithuania continued to preoccupy Pilsudski and Beck. There had been, intermittently, unofficial contacts initiated by Poland or Lithuania. When no results were achieved Pilsudski felt frustrated in his hopes. He had journeyed to Geneva and had forced the Lithuanian representative to concede that a state of peace existed between Poland and Lithuania, and yet no diplomatic, cultural, or economic relations had resulted. In 1930, Pilsudski dropped his efforts to achieve a settlement.[38]

As long as antagonism existed between Poland and Germany or between Poland and Russia, Lithuania had no need to worry about her relations with Poland. Germany or Russia would back her in the event she was threatened by Poland. But when this protection was nullified by the nonaggression system that Poland had built up, unofficial agents of Lithuania began to appear in Warsaw. Pilsudski, regarding this method of dealing as not befitting the dignity of states, refused to negotiate with these agents and demanded that the Lithuanian Government send fully empowered emissaries. When the Lithuanians could reach no decision on this point, he tried to facilitate such a step and, under various pretexts, sent to Kaunas first Anatol Muhlstein, Minister-Counselor in Paris, and later Alexander Prystor, former Prime Minister. The Lithuanians demanded a token declaration concerning Vilna, which Pilsudski was not inclined to make. However, Prystor's talks with Smetona, the President of Lithuania, apparently led to a draft arrangement that would establish normal relations between the two countries.[39]

At this stage, a new factor interfered—the Eastern Pact negotiations. They engendered a tendency in the three Baltic states—Latvia, Estonia, Lithuania—to keep closely together. A new "Baltic Entente" resulted from the meeting the three governments held in Kaunas at the beginning of July, 1934. It was to be expected that their reasserted solidarity would receive full approval from Poland, since Beck had repeatedly proclaimed that they could count on Poland's help—even without any agreement—so long as they were willing to defend their political independence and territorial integrity.[40]

Beck paid official visits to Tallinn and Riga in July, 1934, in connection with French-Soviet efforts regarding the Eastern Pact. Contrary to certain suspicions, Beck did not attempt to impose a negative attitude toward the pact upon the Estonian and Latvian governments. He anticipated, however, that an exchange of information on the inherent problems would help these governments evaluate the dangers implicit in Russian preponderance within the system of the Eastern Pact.

Apparently Moscow applied counterpersuasion immediately, because on July 30 all three governments issued a joint communiqué proclaiming their full adherence to the projected pact. Moreover, the newly opened channels between Kaunas and Warsaw were closed. So it is not surprising that Beck, in conversations with Barthou, expressly sought to exclude Lithuania from the pact.[41]

His Baltic policy, pursued in his visits to Estonia and Latvia in 1934 and 1938 and to Sweden and Norway in 1938, was an attempt to turn the clock back and to link together in a vertical line the states separating Russia and Germany. Their solidarity under Poland's leadership would either eliminate the threat of war or pave the way for a common defense.

The other obstacle to Polish support of the Eastern Pact was her relations with Czechoslovakia.

Despite the efforts of Skirmunt and Skrzynski and the signing of agreements intended to settle old disputes, the relations between the two countries did not improve greatly. Their divergence in political concepts and viewpoints was most apparent in Geneva, where Benes played a prominent role. Contrary to the opinions expressed by several writers, envy did not motivate Polish statesmen in their criticism and generally negative estimation of Benes and his untiring activity. Beck even had a sort of admiration for the ability of the Czechoslovakian Foreign Minister to intervene in almost all current international problems. Still, he found Benes' constant interference rather exasperating. Benes' frequent efforts to promote a viewpoint favorable to the Soviets and his submissiveness to French wishes often collided with Polish policies. The Polish Foreign Minister could not be sure whether Benes' declarations of his readiness to cooperate with Poland indicated a change in Czechoslovak policy or were merely tactical moves. The Four-Power Pact, in which Benes changed the attitude of the Little Entente, demonstrated the flexibility of his opinions.

Despite Beck's statement to Barthou in Warsaw that the mistreatment of the Polish minority was the cause of the rift between Poland and Czechoslovakia, its roots went deeper.[42] The Poles could not overlook the Czechs' pan-Slavic sympathies. They remembered Czechoslovakia's opposition to Polish sovereignty over eastern Galicia, its acquisition of Ruthenia as a territorial extension toward Russia, and its support of Ukrainian organizations opposing Polish-Ukrainian understanding. They regarded Czech subservience to Soviet aims as a latent danger to Poland.

Benes immediately and wholeheartedly accepted the Eastern Pact concept of a French-Soviet framework for integrating the

East Central European and Baltic nations. This was contrary to the Polish outlook. Beck, in his conversations with French statesmen, objected to such a system because it would endanger the equilibrium so laboriously created by Polish efforts in the very same area. In regard to Czechoslovakia, he did more. He reserved his opinion on her participation, believing that she belonged not to the territory in question but to the Danubian area.[43] Since Rumania was not included in the French plan, it was difficult to understand why an exception was made of Czechoslovakia and of her alone. The French answer that Czechoslovakia was included because she bordered on Germany clearly showed the specific reason for her participation.

It would have been better for Poland if she had stated her viewpoint clearly and explained her problem to world opinion. But Poland had never had adequate public-relations and foreign-information services. In this respect, the Poles could justly envy the Czechs, who possessed a first-rate propaganda. The Polish viewpoint was never satisfactorily explained or publicized, so that Poland's foreign policy was often misinterpreted. Yet the reasoning of Pilsudski and Beck was simple. They did not want to commit Poland to one side in the bitter ideological struggle between Germany and the U.S.S.R. They saw the best guarantee of peace in maintaining Poland's stand midway between Moscow and Berlin. This, in their eyes, was a more valuable contribution to peace than building up a mutual-defense group composed of countries with disparate, and in some cases conflicting, interests.

Germany's ostentatious display of friendship for Poland could not fail to create the impression that Polish-German relations were rapidly developing into more than mere neighborliness,[44] and this impression was enhanced in the eyes of foreign observers by the suddenness of the change. Polish public opinion, however, reacted to German overtures with caution and not without suspicion.

It is difficult to understand why within six months Hitler sent two of his most trusted associates and important cabinet members on visits to Warsaw. Perhaps Pilsudski's evasion of the invitation, transmitted by Rauschning, to meet Hitler moved the latter to investigate Polish intentions toward Germany by having his top agents make direct contact with governmental and political circles in Warsaw. Or Beck's journeys and his activities in Geneva and the Baltic capitals might have made the German Government curious as to the Poles' true feelings.

The first to come to Warsaw, in June, 1934, was Goebbels.[45] He skillfully played the role of good-will ambassador, exploring the possibility of reinforcing and broadening German relations with Poland. His visit was ostensibly private in nature. On invitation of the Association for Intellectual Cooperation, he gave a lecture on a high level and in a moderate tone on "National Socialist Germany as a Factor of European Peace." Both Beck and the German Minister invited him to nonofficial receptions, during which he had occasion to talk about politics.

His visit would have been an over-all success, but the effect of his prudent conduct was dissipated when, while he was still in Poland, the Minister of the Interior, Pieracki, was assassinated. The murder was laid to a Ukrainian organization known to have its headquarters in Germany and to be supported by the German authorities. The murderer was suspected to have fled to Germany, whereupon public wrath turned in part against that country.

Another shock of revulsion against Germany struck Poland soon afterward at news of the cruel extermination of the Roehm group. The assassination of Chancellor Dollfuss in an unsuccessful Nazi *coup* in Austria heightened public indignation toward the Hitler regime's methods.[46]

The visit of Goering in January, 1935, was undoubtedly more important to the Germans than that of Goebbels. The ostensible reason was a hunt in the Bialowieza Forest, but, although security measures could account for the secrecy surrounding his arrival and the program for his stay, it now seems certain that the real motivation was a vast political plan conceived by Hitler.

Goering went to Bialowieza with several high-ranking officers of the Polish Army and with Ambassador Lipski and the chief of protocol, who represented the foreign service. Before this audience in the hunting lodge, Goering displayed a grandiose plan for the conquest of Russia by Germany and Poland. According to this fantastic project, Germany would expand into northeast Russia and Poland into the southeast, i.e., the Ukraine. The Poles in the audience were amazed and astonished at this display of rapacious scheming. Lipski suggested to the German Ambassador, von Moltke, that he warn Goering to be less outspoken in his conversations with members of the Polish Government—particularly Pilsudski, whom he was going to see after the hunt. When, despite this warning, Goering spoke of the advantages Poland would obtain by joining Germany in an expedition against Russia, Pilsudski stiffened and evaded any further discussion of this.

Goering's attempts to sound out Poland on her willingness to enter a partnership with Germany were linked to an even larger German concept: creation of a strong anti-Russian group of states, including even England, with the objective of opening for German conquest and colonization large and rich areas, including the oil basins of the Ukraine and the Caucasus. Apparently Hitler had mentioned these plans to the oil magnate Deterding in 1934.[47] If Goering expected a favorable reception from the Poles, he was greatly mistaken. Pilsudski was perfectly aware that in a combination of this kind, the partner was potentially more dangerous than the prospective enemy. Besides, having won the war against Russia in 1920, he saw no reason to start a new one. All he wanted for Poland was peace.

The German plan called, in the initial stage, for an alliance with the projected Ukrainian state. Hence, under the influence of Rosenberg, Hitler started to organize disparate Ukrainian groups into one large national committee. It proved to be impossible to avoid clashes of opinion among the various factions within the committee, and it finally appeared that Soviet agents had infiltrated it.

The reversal in Polish-German relations induced the German Government to change its policy toward the Ukrainians. Up to that time, anti-Polish Ukrainian organizations had found a haven in the three countries where enmity toward Poland and friction with Poland existed, namely Germany, Czechoslovakia, and Lithuania. Thus the Organisaciia Ukrainskih Nacionalistiv (Organization of Ukrainian Nationalists), or OUN, the best-organized party group abroad (under the leadership of Colonel Eugene

Konovalec), had headquarters in Berlin and important sections in Prague and Kaunas. It operated a widespread underground in Poland and was responsible for an attempt on the life of President Wojciechowski and the assassination of Pieracki and Holowko. After the German-Polish declaration was signed and after Hitler conceived his plan for a joint assault with Poland against Russia, the Ukrainian organizations in Germany were advised to stop the anti-Polish activities of their followers in Poland and use them for subversive action across the border in Great Ukraine and other areas of the Soviet Union. This, however, appeared to be more difficult than Hitler had thought. The Polish-Soviet nonaggression treaty enabled the U.S.S.R. to intervene with the Polish Government against Ukrainian activities emanating from Poland and directed toward the territory of the Ukrainian S.S.R.

The Ukrainians in Poland had a strong political organization, the Ukrainian National Democratic Union (UNDO), which had the support of the majority and was well represented in both houses of Parliament. Its ultimate aim was the creation of a Ukrainian state from lands held by the Soviet Union, Poland, Rumania, and Czechoslovakia, but, for the time being, it was demanding only the temporary solution of territorial autonomy in Poland.

The assassination of Pieracki stirred considerable reaction among the Poles and led to restrictive measures against the Ukrainians. Strong controls were imposed on the movements and activities of Ukrainian leaders and agents. Deprived of support by Germany and expecting further restrictions by Polish authorities —without even the possibility of appealing to the League of Nations since Beck's denunciation of the minority procedure—the Ukrainian leadership decided on temporary subsidence and officially disowned the underground movement. The conservative leaders entered into truce talks with the new Minister of the Interior, Koscialkowski, known for his conciliatory attitude toward the Ukrainians. Thus, the position of the Ukrainians in Poland became stationary for a time, and their collaboration with the government and in Parliament brought about a period of calm in Polish-Ukrainian relations.[48]

Goering's indication of the Ukraine as a reward for Poland's collaboration in an assault on the U.S.S.R.[49] was indeed disturbing evidence of Hitler's sweeping designs, but was soon overshadowed by more immediate problems that, in the first months of 1935, demanded the attention of all European governments.

On March 9, Hitler officially informed the world of the existence of a German air force—a fact not unknown to most of the governments. The next Saturday, March 16, he took a more ominous step. Germany reintroduced conscription by decree, putting her armed forces at some 550,000 men. This open repudiation of treaty obligations evoked formal protests from France, England, and Italy. A conference of the three powers at Stresa and a special meeting of the League of Nations Council were announced for the first half of April.

As a signatory of the Versailles treaty, Poland joined the Western powers in condemning the violation. Lipski was instructed to express his government's apprehension that serious complications might arise from the German move.[50] The somewhat involved wording of the protest reflected the ticklish position held by Poland as a result of her nonaggression pledge to Germany. Besides, the German announcement had only confirmed rearmament measures that were already known to France and England but which they had not countered in time despite Pilsudski's endeavors. He did not now expect from them any effective action to block the announced army expansion.[51] He was not mistaken.

The Polish Government, well aware that the possibility of French action depended on England's attitude, viewed with great interest the Berlin visit of Sir John Simon, the British Foreign Secretary, and Anthony Eden, Lord Privy Seal—as well as Eden's journey to Moscow, Warsaw, and Prague. On his way back from Moscow, Eden spent two days in Warsaw, which was the occasion for a frank and extensive exchange of information and opinions. Eden was received by Pilsudski, who, although critically ill, was eager to talk with him and to hear his opinions on Germany and the Soviet Union. Pilsudski attached great importance to establishing closer relations with Great Britain,[52] and he stressed this during his last conversation with Beck, on May 10, two days before his death.[53]

Eden's impression was that Hitler would not adhere to the multilateral assistance pact, and that his goal of complete equality of rights indicated a determination to acquire for Germany everything he could while conceding nothing in return. Hitler's mention of equal German participation in the system of mandates alarmed the British, who saw in it a claim to colonial possessions. His demands for rearmament were exorbitant; he put forward a claim for a German fleet equivalent in strength to 35 per cent of the English Navy. Only a few months later the British Government concluded an Anglo-German naval agreement based on that very ratio.

From his conversations in Moscow, Eden had concluded that the U.S.S.R. had neither the intention nor the capability of undertaking aggressive actions and would not for a long time.[54] The Soviet leaders feared Germany's massive rearmament and wanted to conclude a mutual security pact, even without Poland and Germany. According to Soviet observations, there were two schools of thought in Germany. The Nazis, in power, sought expansion to the east, while the Reichswehr favored an attack on the west in order to be free to expand to the east afterward.[55] Neither Beck nor Pilsudski shared Eden's evaluation of Soviet strength; they believed he greatly underestimated it.

Eden's conversations in Warsaw with Beck and other officers of the Polish Foreign Ministry were cordial and sincere. Beck gave him a complete account of the objectives of Polish foreign policy and cited his objections to the Eastern Pact. Their explanations made it clear that Poland would be favorably disposed toward any new international project that would neither jeopardize the political equilibrium she had reached with her neighbors nor undermine the authority of the League of Nations.[56]

Beck advised Eden of the imminent visit of Laval, who had been invited by the Polish Government to stop in Warsaw at the beginning of May on his way to Moscow.

Meanwhile, at the Stresa conference and the special meeting of the League of Nations Council, the great powers proved beyond doubt their unwillingness to oppose German rearmament. The Stresa conference, sponsored by Mussolini and attended by dele-

gates of France, England, and Italy, produced merely a communiqué asserting that complete agreement had been reached on all
questions discussed. Only one point was clearly stated: the decision to defend Austria's independence. The resolution submitted
to the Council by the same three powers was not substantially different. It was virtually limited to the statement that Germany had
violated treaty obligations, thereby threatening the security of Europe, and that her action deserved condemnation. Several members of the Council criticized the draft, but, aware that to reject
the resolution would be to support Hitler, they decided that "to
acquiesce was the lesser evil." [57]

Poland's vote in support of the anti-German resolution proposed
by the three great powers had a favorable effect on Franco-Polish
relations.[58] On the eve of Laval's visit, such a *détente* was most
welcome.

Laval arrived in Warsaw on May 10, after signing a mutual-
assistance pact with Potemkin, U.S.S.R. Ambassador in Paris. The
purpose of his visit was to explain certain facets of the Franco-
Russian pact and to discuss plans for a multilateral pact of nonaggression and consultation.

In spite of Laval's assurances that the treaty with the Soviet
Union did not affect Franco-Polish relations, Poland regarded it
as a blow to the alliance. The pact provided for mutual help in
case of aggression against one of the signatories by a European
power (*i.e.*, Germany), in accordance with the Covenant of the
League of Nations. It was open to participation by Poland, the
Baltic states, and Germany. Beck had explained Poland's reasons
for not joining such a system in his talks with Barthou in 1934, and
now he repeated them for Laval. Laval emphasized that the new
project for a multilateral nonaggression pact was not directed
against Germany and was open to all interested countries, including the Reich and the U.S.S.R. Beck's response was noncommittal.
He explained the necessity of a thorough examination of all aspects of the new proposal, and stressed Poland's special interests in
northeastern Europe.

Pilsudski was already critically ill, and it was out of the question
for him to see Laval. However, the Franco-Russian pact deeply

disturbed him, and he insisted in his conversations with Beck on the necessity of maintaining and strengthening the alliance with France. In this respect, Laval's visit marked a step forward. The Poles' efforts to make it a success were appreciated by the French, who regarded them as proof of Poland's continuing friendship.

Laval left Warsaw hardly expecting to be back in Poland within so few days to represent his country at Pilsudski's funeral. On the evening of May 12, the day of Laval's departure, Józef Pilsudski, first Marshal of Poland, passed away, exactly nine years after his *coup d'état*.

The funeral ceremonies in Warsaw and Kraków were a manifestation of the great grief that swept the whole Polish nation. Their solemn character was deepened by the presence of many foreign special missions. France was represented by Laval and Marshal Pétain, Germany by Goering, and Rumania by Marshal Presan. Laval and Goering took advantage of this unexpected meeting by holding a political conversation that lasted more than two hours and was important to Hitler's foreign policy.

Pilsudski did not leave a political testament. The only recommendation he made shortly before his death was that General Smigly-Rydz should succeed him as Inspector General of the army, and immediately after Pilsudski's death President Moscicki signed a decree to that effect. No changes were made in the composition of the government, but, owing to the enactment of the new constitution on April 23, the President's role became more important and conspicuous.[59]

Work on a new constitution had started soon after the *coup* of 1926 and was performed entirely by members of the governmental majority, the opposition parties having refused to participate. The intention was to preserve the system of parliamentary democracy, while considerably increasing the authority and powers of the chief executive.[60] The President of the Republic was thus assigned the role of arbiter; his function was to assure the smooth cooperation of the various branches of the government and to reconcile their viewpoints. The Constitution maintained the principles of cabinet responsibility to the parliament and of universal suffrage. However, the laws enacted in July, 1935, vitiated the electoral system, restricting the tickets to candidates presented by select groups of citizens and eliminating party competition. The members of the Senate—one-third of whom were to be nominated by the President—were also determined by a complicated system of electoral colleges of limited composition. In spite of these features, the new state structure was not authoritarian or totalitarian. The Parliament, although restricted, still exercised a controlling and censuring role.

The Constitutional Law of April 23 was passed because the opposition parties abstained from voting and because of the surprise tactics employed by the party in power. This provoked strong criticism from the opposition and from a large section of the nation. Nonetheless, those who had fashioned the new constitution had sought to eliminate the excesses of parliamentary factions and the influence of unscrupulous politicians. They endeavored, perhaps in no very realistic manner, to establish a middle course between extreme parliamentary prerogatives and excessive executive control.

No struggle for power took place after Pilsudski's death. The legal as well as the actual structure of the state was maintained by tacit agreement of the whole nation. This was the greatest tribute rendered to the memory of the man who had centered his life efforts on Poland's revival, the reconstruction of the Polish state, and the elimination from the national life of the evil consequences of the past, and who, in so doing, had raised Poland to a position of importance among European nations.

V

The Policy of Equilibrium: 1935–39

THE DEATH OF Marshal Pilsudski deprived the regime he had established of its guide in foreign affairs. Beck had formulated and directed the details of foreign policy, but it was Pilsudski who had set the course. Beck had referred to him all questions of importance and had discussed with him the measures and decisions to be taken. His faith in Pilsudski's exceptional ability to penetrate the intricate pattern of international affairs had moved him to follow his advice scrupulously. This close collaboration and frequent consultations with Pilsudski had given Beck an intimate familiarity with the late Marshal's ideas in foreign affairs.

In spite of some opposition to his policy among men high in the government, he had enjoyed the support and full confidence of the President of the Republic. President Moscicki was aware that Beck was the only man within the governmental inner circle who could continue Pilsudski's foreign policy. Beck's personal ambition was counterbalanced by his strong patriotism and his dedication to his great task. It was these qualities, combined with a brilliant intelligence and dynamic energy, that had led Pilsudski to entrust him with the conduct of foreign affairs.[1] An additional reason for retaining Beck was his identification with the change in relations between Poland and Germany and the conclusion of the Polish-German declaration of nonaggression. The appointment of a new foreign minister would probably be interpreted in Germany as a shift of policy.

In fact, shortly after Pilsudski's death, closer cooperation with France was advocated by General Smigly-Rydz. The new Inspector General and his advisers insisted on the necessity of improving relations with France. Their position was motivated by two weighty factors. First, the army, faced with the massive rearmament of the German and Russian armies, urgently required modern war matériel. The high-ranking officers, most of them trained by French instructors and influenced by French doctrines, quite naturally desired to obtain the necessary help and equipment from France. Second, it was urgently necessary to improve and enlarge Poland's industrial production, as much for economic and social reasons as for military ones. This induced the economists and military leaders to look toward France in search of capital that Poland could not supply.[2]

The Germans knew that the policy of *rapprochement* with the Reich had many opponents in Poland. They were afraid that after the death of Pilsudski changes would take place in Poland's foreign policy,[3] especially since European opinion had reacted to Hitler's rearmament decree with dismay and condemnation. In England, in spite of the government's policy of good will, evidenced by the visit of Simon and Eden to Berlin, public opinion strongly disapproved Germany's violation of her obligations. The common front at the Stresa conference contributed further to the uneasiness, even alarm, prevailing in Germany.

To reassure the world, Germany wished to exploit her friendly relations with Poland. It was for this reason that, in his speech of May 21, Hitler stressed the importance of this relationship and praised the role of the late Marshal Pilsudski in forming a *détente* between the two nations. Anxious to placate world opinion and to mitigate the misgivings of the great powers, Hitler sought to create the impression of moderation. Soon afterward, on June 18, the Anglo-German naval agreement revealed the success of his tactics. The common front of Stresa had been destroyed.

Beck decided to pay a visit to Berlin to clarify Hitler's true intentions toward Poland and to eliminate any existing doubts and apprehensions. His visit, on July 3 and 4, gave him an opportunity to contact the most important members of the German Government and the German Army. Hitler assured him of Germany's determination to develop the friendly relations with Poland initiated in January, 1934. Beck assured the Fuehrer that Polish policy would follow the course laid down by Pilsudski, and that Poland would maintain friendly relations with Germany. He also intimated that Polish-Soviet relations were satisfactory—an indication that Poland would not be drawn into Hitler's anti-Russian schemes.[4]

Beck's visit had an effect on Polish-Danzig relations, which always reflected the relationship between Berlin and Warsaw. It had been a guiding principle of Polish policy to avoid official discussion of Danzig with Germany, but, since Hitler's authority actually determined the Free City's policy, unofficial Polish-German contacts had been used to resolve difficulties involving crucial decisions.

In May, 1935, a serious crisis arose because of the devaluation by the Danzig Senate of the local currency—the *gulden*—and the resulting necessity of introducing control of foreign currencies, including Polish legal tender. This led to the freezing of considerable Polish funds. Countermeasures by Poland and then retaliatory moves by Danzig brought about severe tension. The situation, if prolonged, would detach Danzig from Poland economically and connect it firmly to Germany.

There were reasons to believe that the Wilhelmstrasse, in order to counteract the *détente* between Poland and Germany, backed the action of Danzig, which was instigated by reckless nationalists. But Beck's visit to Berlin brought about the desired result.[5] At the height of the crisis, after Ambassador Lipski intervened with Goering and Hitler, those responsible for the "intrigue" were ordered to re-establish the economic situation that had existed prior to the dispute. Thus, a Polish-German conflict over Danzig was avoided, and in August, 1935, Poland and the Free City reached a compromise on financial questions.

The journey to Berlin had supplied Beck with valuable information and convinced him of the stability of Hitler's regime. Because of the political importance of this visit, Beck's own situation within the Polish Government was strengthened. For Hitler, it was important, too. It not only allowed him to display peaceful intentions, but was exploited to improve Germany's international position, which had already been strengthened by developments among the Western powers.

As a result of League of Nations sanctions against Italy, which

PENNSYLVANIA MILITARY COLLEGE
CHESTER, PENNSYLVANIA
LIBRARY

had violated the Covenant by invading Ethiopia, the Italian Government withdrew from its close association with England and France. Despite their efforts to placate him, Mussolini reversed his policy and ceased to oppose Germany's expansionist plans in Central Europe. Italy's withdrawal from the League of Nations and her growing solidarity with Germany led eventually to creation of the Axis.

Poland, a noncolonial power, was not directly interested in the Italo-Ethiopian conflict. Polish public opinion condemned the aggression against Ethiopia, but traditional sympathy for Italy softened its disapproval. The government's attitude was dictated by the conviction that a rift in the Western camp would have most undesirable repercussions in European politics. Hence, in the League of Nations discussions, the Polish delegation exerted a conciliatory influence, and Beck accepted membership in the Committee of Five, set up to investigate possibilities of a peaceful solution. When League action failed to prevent war and economic sanctions were applied against Italy, Poland complied with them.[6] She was, however, among the first nations to revoke them when, in July, 1936, the League decided to bring them to an end.

The Assembly session of September, 1935, which dealt with the Ethiopian question, also had to elect new members to the Council. Poland's term had come to an end, and Beck decided, in spite of his disillusionment with the League, to seek re-election to the Council seat. He was anxious to prove that no change in foreign policy had occurred in Poland after the death of Pilsudski. The semipermanent seat of Poland was renewed by a larger number of votes than on either previous occasion.[7]

The year 1936 opened propitiously for the Polish Foreign Minister. During the January session of the League's Council, the Danzig questions, which at first seemed to presage serious troubles, were settled smoothly. This was in large part due to the friendly attitude of the British delegate, Anthony Eden. Because England was the most important member of the Committee of Three dealing with Danzig questions, Beck considered close personal relations with Eden of fundamental importance. Previous contacts between the two men had prepared the ground for mutual confidence and understanding, which were strengthened during the Council session and resulted in a profitable cooperation.

Long convinced that Poland's international position would be greatly improved by closer ties with Great Britain, Beck had discreetly and consistently worked toward this goal.[8] As soon as he had been appointed Undersecretary of State in 1930, he had made an exploratory, unofficial visit to London. In the course of the nine years during which he played a leading role in Polish foreign policy, he took advantage of every occasion to improve Anglo-Polish relations, to explain to British statesmen the fundamentals that shaped Poland's position, and the reasons for his own political moves. The weakness of France and the growing might of Germany induced him to seek in England a basis of support for the security of Poland.

An opportunity for direct contact with leading British statesmen arose in March, 1936, when the League of Nations Council convened in London to discuss another German violation of international obligations. Hitler, in ordering his army to occupy the demilitarized Rhineland province on March 7, had violated not only the Versailles treaty but also the Rhine Pact, solemnly and voluntarily signed in 1926. Hitler's pretext was that the Franco-Soviet treaty, approved by the French Chamber of Deputies on February 27, was incompatible with the Locarno treaties and consequently invalidated them.

None of the other signatories of Locarno accepted this interpretation; they were convinced, on the contrary, that the military reoccupation of the Rhineland had created a clear *casus foederis* that should have produced immediate military measures by France and immediate support of such French action by the guarantors and parties to the Locarno agreements. The Franco-Polish treaty, concluded within this system, established a clear obligation of mutual assistance. Poland attached great importance to the fulfillment of this reciprocal pledge. On March 7, Beck asked the French Ambassador to call on him and solemnly gave him positive assurance that Poland stood ready to honor her commitment to France.[9] On the same day, Beck made a declaration to the Belgian

Ambassador, concluding with "if Belgium should march, we shall march immediately too." [10]

Beck offered these spontaneous assurances after consultation with the President and General Smigly-Rydz. He was probably skeptical of developments in the West, recalling that France had failed to react to previous German infringements. However, because this violation was so flagrant and because Great Britain and Italy had provided guarantees at Locarno, it was assumed that the French Government would immediately order a forceful military demonstration on the Rhine.[11]

Berlin also anticipated an armed reaction by the Western powers, and military circles foresaw the possibility of a withdrawal of German troops. But Hitler had been a better judge of the French and British. His dramatic appeal to the German people and his promise to the West of immediate and lasting solutions to international problems succeeded in misleading public opinion, particularly in England.[12] Consultations between Paris and London were abortive. Their sole result was the formal protests made by the French and British ambassadors in Berlin and the convocation of the League of Nations Council in London, in conformity with the Rhine Pact.[13]

"The meeting in London seemed to be, for the first time in the history of the Council, a gathering of individual states possessing no common legal or moral basis of action, but each concerned with its own particular interests in relation to the resurgent German power. . . ." [14] Beck found himself in a difficult position. The Locarno powers were endeavoring to settle the question within their own small circle; after the Council concluded that Germany had violated the Locarno treaty by occupying the Rhineland, the Western powers drafted proposals and handed them to Ribbentrop. Only then was the text presented officially to the Council. This procedure aroused the opposition of the smaller powers in the Council, who were determined to prevent a recurrence of what had happened at Stresa.[15] Beck played a prominent role in resisting the great powers' imposition of their decisions on the Council. His opposition to this and his criticism of the Locarno treaty were strongly resented by the French delegation. His relations with other statesmen, however, particularly Eden and van Zeeland, were informative and cordial. He was left with an impression of widespread deterioration of international relations.

It would seem that Poland's spontaneous backing of her ally in the declaration of March 7 should improve Franco-Polish relations. But in London the personal contacts between Beck and the head of the French delegation, Premier Flandin, left much to be desired. Fortunately Paul-Boncour was among the French delegates, and the good offices of this tested friend of Poland prevented the change in the international situation from affecting the Franco-Polish alliance. Actually, Hitler had invalidated the Locarno treaties, and—although the other Locarno powers continued to consider themselves bound by them—this jeopardized the Franco-Polish guarantee agreement. Poland therefore wanted France to reaffirm the bilateral alliance of 1921.[16] Negotiations produced written assurances by the French Government that the 1921 agreements were still in full force. Thus, as a result of Germany's breach of treaty provisions, Franco-Polish relations were clarified and their mutual-assistance obligations strengthened.

But this result, no matter how beneficial to Poland, could in no way compensate for the infinitely more serious consequences of France's weakened position and the diminishing of the alliance's potentialities. It is obvious that cooperation between the French and Polish armies in the event of German aggression would be made more difficult and more complicated by the remilitarization of the Rhineland, specifically the building of the Siegfried Line.

The withdrawal of France from the Rhine had lessened her political influence in Europe. Germany's prestige, on the contrary, had grown with Hitler's triumph over the Western powers. In the Danubian and East Central European areas, the French defensive system was weakened, and Germany's political and economic influence became more decisive.

Because of the ideological strife between Communism and Nazism, the U.S.S.R., after her reappearance in world politics in the early thirties, might have become the center of opposition to Hitler's expansionist plans. But the aversion of the East Central

European nations to Communist doctrine and to the Soviets' ruthless suppression of human liberties excluded this possibility. Moreover, the extensive purges of Russian military and political leaders in 1936–37 were believed to have considerably weakened the Soviet Union.

Poland's foreign policy, which consistently strove to maintain parallel and equal relations with each of her two powerful neighbors without committing herself to either, had to make up for the loss of security produced by France's failure to stand up to Hitler. The smaller powers of East Central and Eastern Europe were in danger of being forced to participate in the struggle between Nazi dynamism and Communist imperialism, which was expected to culminate in a momentous clash. Their common danger drew them closer together as they endeavored to retain their neutrality. These circumstances induced Beck to make efforts to strengthen Poland's position by organizing a "region of security" with Warsaw as a center. With this in mind, he established closer links with the Scandinavian and Baltic countries as well as with Yugoslavia and Hungary and paid an official visit to Rome. His first step in organizing this security region concerned Rumania, whose unsatisfactory relations with Poland urgently called for improvement.

In spite of an alliance, steadfastly endorsed by both nations, their cooperation in international politics was lacking in continuity and frankness. On more than one important foreign political problem, Beck and Titulescu, the respective foreign ministers, did not see eye to eye. A faithful follower of French initiatives and suggestions, a supporter of the League of Nations, in which he played a prominent role, and a warm advocate of the Little Entente, Titulescu disapproved Beck's policy of pursuing bilateral rather than multilateral agreements.[17] Yet their divergent viewpoints would not have unfavorably influenced relations between the two governments had they not disagreed on policy toward Soviet Russia.

As will be recalled, Polish diplomacy in the past had constantly promoted a simultaneous negotiation and conclusion of agreements with the U.S.S.R. by all her western neighbors. Poland was particularly interested in Rumania's participation in the various stages of development of a security system with the Soviet Union. Thus, thanks to Polish efforts, Rumania became a signatory of the Litvinov Protocol of 1928. In 1931, the Soviet Union, prompted by Japan's expansionist designs in China and the desire to increase her security in the west, resumed talks with Poland aimed at concluding a nonaggression treaty. In the preliminary talks, Moscow agreed without objection to simultaneous negotiations with the Baltic states and Rumania. But Titulescu's persistent demand that the treaty provide for surrendering *de jure* Russian rights to Bessarabia rendered progress impossible. The compromise efforts of Zaleski, at the time Polish Foreign Minister, were of no avail. The Polish Government finally decided to sign the treaty with the U.S.S.R. without the participation of Rumania. Finland, Latvia, and Estonia concluded similar agreements. The Polish-Soviet treaty's provision that all former Polish obligations should remain in force attested to Poland's loyalty and candor in her relations with Rumania.

The dissatisfaction of Polish diplomacy with Titulescu's delays and evasions was somewhat relieved when in July, 1933, Rumania, with Russia's other western neighbors, joined the U.S.S.R. in signing the Convention for the Definition of Aggression. But further efforts by the Polish Government to bring about normal relations between Moscow and Bucharest were unsuccessful.[18]

Titulescu's policy changed radically in 1934 when France launched her plan for an Eastern Pact: Reversing his former attitude, he established diplomatic relations with the U.S.S.R. When France concluded a mutual-assistance treaty with the Soviet Union and Czechoslovakia followed her example, Titulescu embarked upon a campaign aimed at Rumania's participation in this fragmentary "Eastern Locarno." His policy was disapproved by the King and other influential leaders in Rumania. Since Titulescu's international and domestic prestige was considerable, Poland was apprehensive lest his opinions should prevail and render worthless the Polish-Rumanian alliance, directed specifically against Soviet aggression. The situation changed when Titulescu stepped down as Foreign Minister in August, 1936.[19] As early as September, his successor, Victor Antonescu, paid a visit to Warsaw, where the policies of both allies were satisfactorily adjusted. There followed a series of exchange visits by both allies and manifestations of cooperation, culminating in a journey to Bucharest, in June, 1937, of President Moscicki, shortly thereafter reciprocated by a visit to Warsaw of King Carol. On this occasion, it was decided to raise the diplomatic missions to embassies. This reversal in Rumania's foreign policy, followed by the King's assumption of almost dictatorial powers, especially in the field of foreign relations, provoked a resentment in Moscow that lasted until the outbreak of World War II.[20]

Another action undertaken by Polish diplomacy in the Danubian area concerned Yugoslavia. In general, Poland's foreign political activities were limited to the area of her immediate or important interests, in accordance with Pilsudski's warning against involvement beyond those limits. No close links existed with Yugoslavia, whose geopolitical situation differed greatly from that of Poland. Nevertheless, similar attitudes toward postwar problems, parallel tactics in questions discussed in Geneva, especially minority problems, and a common interest in maintaining the *status quo* created by the Paris peace treaties occasionally motivated amicable cooperation. A treaty of friendship had been concluded as early as September, 1926, and in 1931, Voislav Marinkovitch, Yugoslavia's able Minister of Foreign Affairs, paid an official visit to Warsaw, where he and Zaleski signed a convention on cultural cooperation. The assassination of King Alexander of Yugoslavia in 1934 unfortunately interrupted the development of these relations. The violent resentment of the Yugoslavs was directed against Hungary, which was accused of having favored the terrorist group alleged to have inspired this crime. Poland, because of her traditional friendship with Hungary, was also viewed with bitterness. It was essential to eliminate the resulting coolness in Polish-Yugoslav relations in order to maintain stability in East Central Europe despite France's weakened position.

Polish diplomacy undertook this task early in 1935. A more active Polish program of economic and cultural cooperation, as well as developments in the domestic affairs of Yugoslavia, led to elimination of the grievances and a fruitful exchange of ideas and information. The long-overdue visit of the Polish Foreign Minister to Belgrade, reciprocating Marinkovitch's journey to Warsaw, was made in May, 1936. It restored candid relations between the two countries, and later helped Poland to promote understanding between Yugoslavia and Hungary. Beck's conversations with Yugoslav leaders convinced him of the similarity of Polish and Yugoslav attitudes toward the politics of the great powers.[21]

Of much greater importance than the steps taken by Poland in the Danubian area was the improvement in Franco-Polish relations. After almost two years of marked coolness between Paris and Warsaw, caused mainly by Poland's reluctance toward the French Eastern Pact plan, both sides made efforts to improve relations. During Flandin's premiership, no improvement resulted from Beck's spontaneous declaration of solidarity on March 7 in the face of the German military occupation of the Rhineland.[22] But the new French Government under the premiership of Léon Blum, with Yvon Delbos as Foreign Minister, undertook to strengthen its ties with the nations of East Central Europe to off-set Germany's improved strategic position. The efforts to intensify relations with Poland resulted in reciprocal visits of high military personnel. General Gamelin, Chief of Staff of the French Army, visited Warsaw, and the Inspector General of the Polish Army, General Smigly-Rydz, was invited to participate in French maneuvers in the summer of 1936. Extensive talks on military matters took place, and a loan agreement was concluded.[23] No political conditions were attached. Poland obtained 2 billion francs, partly in cash and partly in matériel. In spite of the devaluation of the French currency soon thereafter, the loan contributed greatly to the stability of the zloty and development of heavy industry in Poland. The military talks, according to Gamelin's memoirs and Polish sources, did not result in specific arrangements for concerted action in the event of German aggression but rather in an exchange of information.[24] Despite the efforts of Noël,[25] the French did not ask for Beck's dismissal nor did they raise the question of Polish-Czechoslovak relations. Thus, contrary to Noël's expectations, the visit of General Smigly-Rydz to France indirectly strengthened Beck's position, since the reinforcement of Franco-

Polish ties was regarded as the consequence of the Foreign Minister's general policy. For Smigly-Rydz, the Rambouillet arrangements were a personal and political success, which brought him in November the marshal's baton.

To allay any German apprehension that the negotiations between the military chiefs of France and Poland might bring about a change in Poland's foreign policy, Beck delegated the Undersecretary of State to Berlin, on the convenient pretext of representing Poland at the Olympic Games. Count Szembek, known for his prudent but favorable attitude toward cooperation with Germany, took full advantage of the lavish ceremonies and brilliant social gatherings to talk extensively with German officials.[26] He had discussed his arguments in advance with Beck and now adapted them so skillfully for each individual that he convinced the German leaders of the stability and continuity of Poland's attitude toward Germany. Thus, the strengthening of Franco-Polish bonds did not exert the detrimental effect on Polish-German relations that might have been feared. Beck's position was further consolidated.

Szembek also faced the task of sounding out German leaders on the Danzig problems that constantly troubled the Polish Government. At this time, a serious conflict had broken out between the Senate of the Free City and the League of Nations' High Commissioner.

Although the absence, since 1934, of Polish-Danzig controversies in the League of Nations Council had considerably eased Poland's position in Geneva, the repeated attempts of the Nazi Party to violate the Statute of the Free City had led to a situation making it necessary for the Polish Government to take a stand against the Danzig administration and thus against German policies. Because of her rights in Danzig, as well as her membership in the Council, Poland had to oppose the Nazification of the Free City. Danzig had become the touchstone of Polish-German relations, and the Polish attitude was bound sooner or later to create tension in those relations.

Beck faced a harsh dilemma during the July, 1936, session of the Council when it discussed the report submitted by the League's

High Commissioner in Danzig, Sean Lester.[27] Besides complaints about the administration's unconstitutional discrimination against opposition groups and the Jewish community, Lester reported an incident involving the prestige of both himself and the League. During a three-day visit of the German cruiser "Leipzig" in the port of Danzig, her captain failed to pay him the customary official visit—reportedly on orders of the German Government. During the Council's discussion of Lester's report, Greiser, the President of Danzig's Senate, behaved in an unusually aggressive and disrespectful manner, arousing amazement and indignation. To resolve this delicate situation, the Council requested Poland, which was in charge of Danzig's external affairs, to obtain satisfaction for the League.[28]

Since Germany's prestige was involved—and also Hitler's, as Commander in Chief of the armed forces—the task was extremely ticklish. A compromise was worked out, after arduous negotiations conducted by the Polish Ambassador in Berlin, under which Germany, in an exchange of notes with Warsaw, stated that she had no intention of violating Danzig's Statute or the rights of Poland in the Free City.

At its September session, the Council took note of the compromise and the case was closed. Lester's situation, however, remained precarious and he finally resigned. A Swiss historian and diplomat, Professor Burckhardt, succeeded him in February, 1937.

In a tense atmosphere in which the contradictory interests and ambitions of Germany, Poland, and the League might at the slightest provocation trigger an international conflict, Professor Burckhardt played a moderating role. He had easy access to the governments and parties involved. Through his friendship with the German Secretary of State, Weizsäcker, he had a unique opportunity for direct contact with German authorities, including Hitler. The Polish Government maintained continuously good relations with him. But the decline of the League, the growing expansionism of Germany, and the unwillingness of England and France to check the developments in Danzig had already paved the way for its conversion into a totalitarian structure. In spite of his ability and his use of flexible methods, Burckhardt became somewhat of a passive witness to the gradual assimilation of Danzig's political structure to that of the Reich.

During his tenure of office,[29] Poland's relations with Danzig became more and more complicated and difficult. Free access to the sea, for valid reasons regarded by Poland as indispensable to her sovereignty, could be secured only by the full exercise of Poland's rights in Danzig. The dynamism and ruthlessness of Nazism, introduced into the Free City's domestic policy, were by their very nature opposed to Polish interests and aims, but good relations with Germany required the Polish Government to refrain from interference in the problems of the German population of Danzig. When Polish rights were violated, Beck endeavored to exert an indirect influence by appropriate steps in Berlin. Otherwise, he could only observe and evaluate the intentions of Germany in Danzig's problems. The very intricacy of this situation inclined the Polish Minister to believe the repeated and categorical assurances of Hitler and Goering that Poland's rights in Danzig and the Statute of the Free City would be respected and that "nothing would happen in Danzig against Poland." [30]

The German Government's true intentions concerning Danzig have been revealed by the publication, among the documents of the Nuremberg trial, of Weizsäcker's confidential memorandum of October, 1936. Its opinions and conclusion are diametrically opposed to the official statements and assurances so loudly expressed by German statesmen during that period.[31] Beck, despite his shrewdness and distrust, was not equal to the guile of the Nazi leaders. But Poland was not the only country to be misled.

In 1936–37, other problems in German-Polish relations required attention, negotiation, and settlement. The Geneva Convention on Upper Silesia, concluded for fifteen years in 1922, was due to expire on July 15, 1937.[32] The German Government approached Warsaw several months before that date with a proposal to replace the minorities-protection section of it with a new bilateral agreement. It would cover the German minority in all of Poland, not only just in Polish Silesia, and an identical system would protect the rights of the Polish minority in Germany.

Beck's declaration before the League of Nations in 1934 had

practically eliminated interference by international organs in Poland's minority problems,[33] and so Poland was disinclined to agree to any new kind of intervention in what it considered domestic problems. Moreover, this bilateral agreement would offer the German Government an opportunity to organize the Germans in Poland according to the Nazi concept of the *Volksgruppe*, whereas the Polish minority in Germany could hardly be expected to profit much. There was no comparison or parallel between the treatment of national minorities in totalitarian Germany and that of ethnic groups in Poland, where, under the Constitution and as a general rule, their rights were recognized and respected. The advantages that the Germans in Poland would acquire would not be counterbalanced by the theoretically similar but actually much lesser gain in rights of the large but economically weak Polish minority in Germany. Hence the dilatory and evasive response by Beck. The Germans, on the other hand, feared that with the expiration of the Geneva Convention and the international institutions it had created, their minority in Poland would forfeit its privileged position.

Berlin gradually increased the pressure for an answer to its proposal. Beck, prodded with insistent reminders, finally presented in Hitler's name, had to yield. However, the agreement took the form of a declaration, not a convention. On November 5, 1937, the day of its publication, representatives of the Polish minority in Germany were received by Hitler, while President Moscicki reciprocated with a much less solemn audience to the German minority leaders in Poland.[34]

At the beginning of 1938, Beck, having been invited with some insistence by the Italian Government, paid a visit to Rome.[35] His conversations with Mussolini and Ciano led him to believe that, although solidarity with Germany was the major consideration in Italy's foreign policy, Il Duce was not uninterested in cautiously and quietly building a bulwark against German penetration into the Balkan and Danubian areas. Yugoslavia, Hungary, Rumania, and Poland would become links in a chain of states serving such a purpose. Since relations between Rumania and Hungary were the most sensitive and dangerous problem in the Danubian area,

Beck and Ciano agreed to unite in efforts to achieve a *rapproche-ment* between Bucharest and Budapest. Poland would exert pressure on the allied Rumanian Government, and Italy would use her influence in Hungary.[36]

This project was in line with Beck's broader plan for a belt of states stretching from the Baltic to the Black Sea that would become a neutral zone between two expansionist powers—Germany and the Soviet Union—and their aggressive ideological warfare, and thus contribute to the preservation of peace.

In his conversations with Italy's dictator, Beck was able to gauge Mussolini's aversion to Communism in general and Soviet activities in Spain in particular. Italy, according to Mussolini, did not seek any territorial advantage or privileged position in Spain, but could not permit the U.S.S.R. to seize the opportunity of the civil war to install and spread Soviet influence in the Mediterranean area.[37]

The Spanish civil war had little impact on Poland's foreign policy. Spain's geographical position was well beyond the area that Poland considered of interest to her. Moreover, the principle of noninterference in the domestic problems of sovereign nations and the determination to keep out of the ideological struggle between Communism and Fascism—two cardinal points of Polish foreign policy—dictated an attitude of neutrality and noncommitment in the Spanish question. But when France and England proclaimed the principle of nonintervention, and measures were taken to insure its application by a supervisory machinery, a clarification of Poland's position became unavoidable. Beck agreed to join in embargo measures, promising that Poland would refrain from selling arms to either side as long as the other participating states abided by the agreement. In Poland, control of military exports was assured because arms were produced by a state-owned industry.

Beck was in Rome when the mounting tension over Austrian problems reached its peak. Ciano and Beck agreed that Schuschnigg's decision to hold a plebiscite—which must have an anti-German character—was a dangerous move, capable of provoking a violent reaction by Hitler. It was obvious to Beck that

Italy would not oppose the *Anschluss;* therefore, since no active opposition could be expected from France and England, Austria was condemned to fall prey to Germany. This occurred a few days after Beck left Rome and while he was still in Italy. He had to cut short his journey and hasten back to Poland, where public opinion had been strongly aroused by the ruthless intimidation and subjugation of an independent nation.[38] But since the great powers had tacitly accepted Austria's integration into the Reich, no other choice was open to Poland.

In a way, the German drive southeastward was favorable to Poland, for it delayed the eastward expansion of Nazi dynamism.[39] But Polish interests certainly suffered from the *Anschluss.* It was brought on by a violation of pledges and show of force that threatened the peace, destroyed the *status quo* established by treaties, and undermined the political stability of Europe. Also, the natural, industrial, and human resources of Austria contributed in no small way to Germany's political and military might, and this was obviously detrimental to Poland.

On the very day that Hitler's troops marched into Austria,[40] Warsaw received news of a serious incident on the Polish-Lithuanian border in which a Polish soldier had lost his life.[41] Amid the nervous tension provoked by the developments in Austria, the press took a serious view of this, and Polish public opinion reacted strongly. Street demonstrations in Warsaw and other cities called for a "march on Kaunas." Beck, returning from Italy on March 14, saw in the tragic incident an opportunity to restore relations between Poland and Lithuania. Continuation of the complete absence of neighborly contacts might present grave dangers in the strained atmosphere caused by German policy. It was decided in high-level government conferences that Poland would serve an ultimatum on Lithuania, its sole objective to be a demand for immediate re-establishment of diplomatic relations, suspended since 1920.

This unusual response to a border incident, accompanied by a concentration of troops in the area of Vilna, created panic in Lithuania and some alarm in the Western capitals. The Lithuanian Government inquired in Paris and London, and Berlin and Moscow, about the attitudes of the respective governments. It received no encouragement to resist the Polish demand; the only offer was that the French and British ambassadors in Warsaw would make inquiries and mild remonstrances with the Polish Government. Failing to gain any modification of the ultimatum, Lithuania decided at length to accept its terms.[42]

Thus the main obstacle to a Baltic bloc was eliminated—unfortunately too late, since Hitler was already secretly planning for the conquest of an eastern *Lebensraum*. But, for the time being, establishment of diplomatic relations led to elimination of the obstacles to normal cooperation between Poland and Lithuania in the political, economic, and cultural fields.

Among the negative aspects of this mostly favorable development was the reaction in various European capitals to Poland's use of coercion—a method intended by Warsaw to save face for Lithuania. Also, the concentration of Polish attention on this emotionally charged problem prevented a full evaluation of the implications of the *Anschluss* as Germany's first step on the road to conquest. How soon Poland herself was to be victimized by Hitler's policy of encirclement can now be seen in subsequently published German documents. The German Government, which was closely watching the Polish-Lithuanian dispute, was already preparing plans to occupy Memel in the event of an armed clash between Poland and Lithuania.[43]

Very shortly after Germany absorbed Austria, a new international crisis broke out, this one concerning Czechoslovakia. At first, the claims of the German population of the Sudeten region, backed by the powerful mechanism of Nazi propaganda, were interpreted as aiming solely at improving that minority's position within the Czechoslovak state. Nor did the gradually increasing frequency of incidents between Sudeten Germans and Czechs give any indication of Hitler's true intentions, which, together with his vast plans of conquest, he had disclosed to only a few of his closest advisers at the secret meeting of November 5, 1937. Hence, the mounting dissatisfaction of the large and well-organized German minority in Czechoslovakia appeared to the world to deserve attention, investigation, and possibly redress. This, too, was the opinion prevailing in Poland. The Polish minority in Czechoslovakia had also encountered numerous difficulties and had been unable to obtain from the Czech authorities recognition of its economic and cultural demands. Its complaints—especially those of the compact group in the two Silesian districts of Teschen and Frysztat, where, according to the prewar Austrian census, the Poles constituted the majority[44]—found a lively, perhaps even a shrill, echo in Poland. Besides, the foreign policy of Czechoslovakia had usually aroused criticism in Polish governmental circles. The 1935 Soviet-Czechoslovak mutual-assistance pact had been vigorously criticized in Poland and looked upon as confirmation that Communist anti-Polish activities were organized in Czechoslovak territory.

As tension over the Sudeten problem grew, Beck began to take a pessimistic view of the future of the Czechoslovak Republic. He had little faith in the strength and will to resist of a state in which a large part of the population, namely the Slovaks and the national minorities, was complaining of being deprived of participation in the government and was being driven into a permanent opposition.[45] With the death of President Masaryk, Czechoslovakia had lost a leader of incontestable authority and outstanding qualities. Beck did not have a high opinion of Benes, his successor.

There is no proof that at the outset of the Czechoslovak crisis Poland desired or even expected a change in the status of Czechoslovakia. Poland's attitude depended upon the action of the Czechoslovak Government as well as upon decisions of the Western powers. But past experience and confidential information inclined the Polish Government to believe that France would not take military measures in defense of Czechoslovakia, that Great Britain would do everything possible to placate Hitler and avoid war, and that the Czechs would yield to German pressure.[46]

Documents published after World War II throw sufficient light on the policy and tactics of the Western powers and the attitude of the Czech Government to show that Poland's evaluation of the situation was sound. It is now known that on July 27, 1938, President Benes proposed to Eisenlöhr, the German Minister in Prague, that "a closer and more lasting" relationship be established between Germany and Czechoslovakia than existed between Poland and Germany.[47] The memoirs of Georges Bonnet have disclosed that Benes later authorized the French and British governments to cede to Germany Czechoslovak territories inhabited by 900,000 to 2 million Germans.[48] This has lately been confirmed by Stefan Osusky, who, having served as Minister of Czechoslovakia in Paris for twenty years, is better qualified than anyone else to know the truth about this proposal.[49]

It is impossible to determine how much Beck's policy in the Czechoslovak crisis was influenced by the above facts, how much by his intuition and foresight, and how much by his reasoning that the multinational Czechoslovak state was, in the long run, condemned either to become a federation of autonomous units or to disintegrate. His not very friendly personal feelings toward the Czechs and their policies might have played a role in his decisions. But it must be remembered that the loss of Teschen in 1920, at a time of mortal danger for the Polish nation, had never been forgotten and was still deeply resented by the Poles, as Paderewski had predicted.[50] The Polish Foreign Minister had to take into account this emotional factor. Although the strategic implications for Poland's security of Germany's unhindered advances into East Central Europe, initiated by the *Anschluss*, did not leave him much choice as to the substance of his policy, the methods he adopted were criticized not only abroad but also in Poland.

Expecting that the German minority would obtain concessions from Czechoslovakia, the Polish Government early put in a claim for equality of treatment for the Polish minority, too. The Czechoslovak Government officially accepted this demand on May 24. The British and French governments, informed of the arrangement, took cognizance of the Czech commitment and expressed their satisfaction with the agreement reached by the two neighboring states.[51] This principle of nondiscrimination, referred to in subsequent notes as "the most-favored nation clause," was from then on regularly put forward by Polish diplomacy both in Prague and in conversations with England and France on the Sudeten problem. When self-determination for the German minority was proclaimed, Poland demanded the same rights for the Poles in

Silesia. When Chamberlain, in his negotiations with Hitler in Berchtesgaden, acquiesced to the cession of the Sudetenland by way of a plebiscite, Poland again sought equality of treatment for the Polish minority. Later Warsaw learned that, as a result of the Anglo-French conference in London on September 19, the outright cession of Sudeten territory with a German majority had been proposed to the Czechoslovak Government. Thereupon, a demand for equality of treatment was put forward by the Polish representatives in the various interested capitals and in the official talks with the French and British ambassadors in Warsaw.[52]

At this point, it was apparent that the Czechoslovak Government would not seriously consider a simultaneous and equal solution of the Polish minority problem. Now, too, the French and British governments were differentiating between the claims of the Germans and those of the Poles and Hungarians in Czechoslovakia.[53] Warsaw interpreted this as a change of policy and resented it as a clear breach of promise.

The turn for the worse in Polish-Czech negotiations was shrewdly exploited by Hitler in his Godesberg negotiations with Chamberlain. Among other arguments, he used the claims of the Polish and Hungarian minorities to raise his demands and to increase tension. This uncalled-for support created the impression of Polish collusion with Germany, an impression that Beck endeavored to remove.[54] His goal was to act independently and in anticipation of Hitler's moves, but without irritating Germany, whose dynamism remained unchallenged by the West.

Warsaw addressed to Prague a formal demand for cession of territory on September 21, immediately after learning that the Czechs had accepted such a solution to the German-minority problem. The Czechoslovak Government answered on September 25, having first asked France and England to intervene in Warsaw in its behalf. The Czech note was considered unsatisfactory, but a letter received at the same time by President Moscicki from President Benes seemed to promise a better outcome. Moscicki's answer was friendly,[55] but on September 27 an official Polish note repeated the demand for immediate cession of parts of Silesia with a Polish majority and for plebiscites in other parts. To avoid complications at a time when Hitler's actions dampened any hope of averting war, the Western powers again intervened. In Warsaw, they sought to restrain Poland from using force; in Prague, the British Minister was instructed to urge the Czechs "to abandon without delay all diplomatic maneuvering." [56] On September 29, the day of the Munich conference, the Polish Government received Prague's answer, dilatory in essence. Thereupon, on September 30, Warsaw delivered a time-limited ultimatum demanding that the Czechoslovak Government take immediate steps to evacuate Teschen and Frysztat and negotiate on pertinent problems.[57]

Again, the great powers undertook concentrated diplomatic steps in Warsaw and Prague. The Czechoslovak Government yielded, persuaded that further opposition would serve no useful purpose. Between October 2 and 12, Polish troops and civil authorities, which had been held in readiness for that task, occupied the Teschen area. At the same time, negotiations were initiated between Prague and Warsaw concerning the rest of the area and technical questions arising from the transfer of sovereignty. Alteration of the border lines without the formerly discussed plebiscite was suggested by the Czechoslovak Government and agreed to. By November 30, all territorial changes had been made, including several minor corrections to the advantage of Czechoslovakia.

The Polish Government's insistence on immediate compliance and the impatience apparent in the rapid succession of diplomatic notes and interventions, including the ultimatum of September 30, were precipitated by the overlapping of Polish and German interests in the Silesian area.

Contrary to appearances and accusations, Poland had entered no agreement with Germany for common action on the cession of Czechoslovak territories.[58] When, in the last days preceding the Munich decisions, it became evident that Hitler would succeed in obtaining the Sudeten area, which included territories bordering on Poland, the Polish Government endeavored to prevent any overlapping of the zones to be occupied by Germany and Poland respectively. The Polish Ambassador in Berlin, Lipski, personally notified Hitler on September 20 of Polish territorial claims, expressly mentioning Teschen, in which Poles constituted a majority, and also Oderberg (Polish Bogumin, Czech Bohumin), a railway junction of great economic and strategic importance to Poland.

After the Godesberg conference, the British Ambassador in Warsaw informed the Polish Ministry of Foreign Affairs of the extent of German territorial demands concerning Silesia and its borders. The so-called "Red Line" on the map Hitler handed to Chamberlain extended well into the Teschen area and gave Germany the vitally important railway junction of Bogumin.[59] The information was transmitted to Lipski, who immediately took up the problem with Weizsäcker. In the course of two conferences on September 28, the latter agreed that Bogumin must be left outside the demarcation line of the German occupation zone. But the Polish Government realized that unless it could obtain immediate cession of the demanded territories, the Germans might reverse their attitude. The problem was actually brought up again on October 4, when the German Undersecretary of State Woerman questioned the agreement, informing Lipski that inclusion of Bogumin in the Polish zone constituted a new and "surprising" fact. Lipski refused to discuss the matter, which had already been decided upon officially. Hitler, to whom the German Foreign Office submitted the problem, decided in favor of the Polish viewpoint.[60]

Her forceful manner in negotiating with Czechoslovakia and her resort to an ultimatum placed Poland in the position of an aggressive and pitiless neighbor. But such actions had been motivated by extremely serious considerations. The agreement reached at the four-power conference in Munich, which did not decide the Polish and Hungarian claims but put off their solution, combined with the prospective guarantee to Czechoslovakia by the Munich powers, might well have deprived Poland of any possibility of realizing her goal concerning Teschen. Moreover, Beck's aversion to a "directorate" of the great powers and the recently demonstrated weakness of England and France in contrast to German expansionism and Hitler's brazenness, caused Beck to fear that Poland's territorial claims might be settled either not at all, or without consulting the Polish Government and to its disadvantage.

It is a matter of conjecture why Benes, who had played such an active role in League of Nations activities, did not appeal to the Council or to the Assembly, which held its annual meeting in the fateful September of 1938. The threat to Czechoslovakia could have initiated a League procedure. However powerless to help, the League still could have served as a sounding board. The German-Czechoslovak case could have been laid before the League, and an open discussion might have had a salutary effect on world public opinion.

An indirect explanation is given by Frank P. Walters in his brilliant work on the League of Nations, when he says that "the Council and the Assembly had now ceased to exercise any shred of political authority." [61] League members were abandoning the Covenant and considered themselves no longer obliged to take automatic action against an aggressor. Litvinov was the only Foreign Minister of a great power to participate in the September session of the Assembly. He took the opportunity to refer to the German-Czechoslovak conflict and to state that the Soviet Government would carry out its obligations toward Czechoslovakia provided France did the same. He suggested applying League procedure to the dispute. No such measure was taken by the Assembly. Realizing that the League was incapable of intervening in the course of events, the other delegations, including the Czechoslovak representative, remained silent on the problem that preoccupied all those present.

On the basis of what was then considered a "realistic" estimate of the League's power and authority, Poland decided to reduce her participation in it. The termination of Poland's three-year term in the Council necessitated re-election by the Assembly if she was to retain her semipermanent seat. It would have been a perfunctory procedure, Poland having been already re-elected three times. But Beck instructed the Polish delegation not to apply for re-election, a lapse that created astonishment and regret among Poland's friends. The Polish Government closed its permanent Delegation to the League and transferred its functions to the Consulate General in Geneva. This, too, was interpreted as a gesture of disregard for the League.

No matter how fully justified was Poland's skepticism about the League, the curtailment of her participation in it was an error. In reapplying for the semipermanent seat in the Council it had occupied for twelve years, the Polish Government would have manifested its adherence to the idea of a gradual organization of human society for the preservation of peace.

Litvinov's attitude and pronouncements at the September, 1938, Assembly reflected Soviet apprehension over the Czechoslovak crisis and the developments in which she had no part. The feeling of isolation, which Poland avoided by enforcing its claims to Teschen, prompted Moscow to manifest its disapproval by certain moves, one of which affected Poland. On September 23, after Poland had presented its demand for territorial adjustment in Prague, the Deputy Commissar for Foreign Affairs, Potemkin, informed the Polish Chargé d'Affaires in Moscow that the U.S.S.R. Government, having learned of Polish troop concentrations on the Czechoslovak frontier, was considering denouncing its nonaggression treaty with Poland.[62] Warsaw sent a cool and curt answer to Moscow the same day. But both governments, unrepresented at the Munich conference, wanted to avoid any deterioration in their mutual relations, and so conversations were soon initiated between Grzybowski, the Polish Ambassador in Moscow, and the Soviet Government. On November 26, a communiqué was published affirming that all treaties already existing between the two countries would continue to govern their relations and emphasizing their determination to observe them faithfully.[63]

This adjustment, after the strained relations created by Poland's policy toward Czechoslovakia, was achieved in line with Poland's constant and persistent effort to equalize its relations with Germany and with the U.S.S.R. Since outwardly, at least, relations with Berlin were developing satisfactorily in spite of the Czechoslovak crisis, Warsaw considered it indispensable to readjust relations with Moscow.

But the equilibrium, seemingly restored, was of short duration. Inevitably, Hitler's plans for expansion would encounter Polish resistance, and the U.S.S.R., never friendly to her western neighbors, would exploit any Polish difficulty to further its own territorial or political aggrandizement. In fact, the temporary, nay futile, character of Poland's attempt to re-establish correct if not amicable relations with her two powerful neighbors was demonstrated barely a few months after the Munich conference.

VI

Toward the World Conflict: 1939

THE LACK OF RESISTANCE to his occupation of Austria—because of Italy's withdrawal from Danubian affairs and the complete passivity of England and France—emboldened Hitler in his plans of conquest. His unopposed annexation of the Sudeten supported his conviction that the Western powers were neither willing nor able to block the expansion of Germany. Now he moved up his timetable for the conquest of *Lebensraum,* which he had disclosed during the secret meeting of November 5, 1937.[1]

As early as November, 1938, the governments of Western Europe had registered and taken seriously various rumors and conjectures about Hitler's plans. They believed that by the spring of 1939 Hitler would start a new adventure. Some reports indicated that he contemplated invading the Netherlands as a preliminary move to paralyze France, threaten England, and gain a free hand for eastward expansion. There was also much talk of German plans to create a vassal Ukrainian state in order to exploit its rich lands for food and raw materials.

It is difficult to determine to what extent these disturbing reports were based on rumors purposely spread by German intelligence and to what extent on reliable information gathered by various diplomatic services. The documents published in connection with the Nuremberg trial indicate that up to the spring of 1939 Hitler had not made up his mind about the sequence of his further aggressions. Only after the dismemberment of Czechoslovakia, when conditions became favorable for an invasion of Poland, did he abandon his previous plan to strike first on the west.

Between October, 1938, and April, 1939, Germany still intended to maintain a tolerable relationship with Poland. World War I had taught Germany to avoid the dangers of a two-front war. Thus Hitler decided to resolve his relations with Poland before he started again on the road to conquest. Apparently he expected, by using means similar to those he had applied so successfully against Czechoslovakia, to obtain an agreement with Poland on Danzig and the Corridor that would make her dependent on Germany's will and ultimately convert her into a German satellite. He would thus obtain a twofold advantage: (1) Poland, despite her alliance with France, could not respond to France's call in the event of German aggression on the west; and (2) Poland's dependence would make her resources available for subsequent German conquest in the east; Danzig and the Polish lines of communication from west to east would complete the existing East Prussian facilities for disposition of military forces in an assault on the Soviet Union.

On October 24, Ribbentrop, having invited Lipski to Berchtesgaden, presented him with a plan for what he called a "global settlement" (*Gesamtlösung*) of Polish-German relations. The main point was a demand for incorporation of Danzig into the Reich and the building of an extraterritorial highway and railroad through Polish Pomerania. As compensation, Germany would extend the declaration of nonaggression for twenty-five years and would guarantee the common frontiers. Ribbentrop also suggested a common policy toward Russia and Poland's joining the anti-Comintern pact.[2] Lipski was bewildered and greatly disturbed by this proposal, which was diametrically opposed to previous German statements. He immediately pointed out that the Nazi leaders, including Hitler, had repeatedly declared that both Danzig and Germany would respect Polish rights in the Free City while Poland refrained from interfering in the affairs of Danzig's German population.[3]

The Polish evaluation of Ribbentrop's proposal can be found in the affidavit submitted by Lipski to the International Military Tribunal in Nuremberg:

In reality the so-called *Gesamtlösung* which Ribbentrop proposed merely boiled down to the wish to open the question of the "Corridor" and the surrender of Danzig to Germany. This was tantamount to severing Poland's access to the sea. The joining of the anti-Comintern pact by Poland would automatically have forced her to give up her treaty of alliance with France, put her at loggerheads with Russia and ultimately drawn her into the orbit of the Nazi policy of conquest.[4]

A half hour after this conversation, Ribbentrop asked Lipski to call on him again, and this time he took up the problem of sub-Carpathian Ruthenia. He suggested a *quid pro quo:* German acceptance of a Polish solution to the Ruthenian problem in return for Polish acceptance of Germany's Danzig proposal.

The Polish Government attached great importance to the question of sub-Carpathian Ruthenia. In the wake of the Munich decisions, Warsaw had to anticipate and, if possible, forestall Germany's efforts to increase her influence and activity in the new Czechoslovakia, especially in Slovakia and Ruthenia. In the latter province, the self-determination principle, revived by Hitler, had found a lively response. Ukrainian groups all over the world demanded self-government for Ruthenia. When it was granted by Prague and sub-Carpathian Ruthenia became a federal part of Czechoslovakia, in October, most Ukrainians in Western Europe and in the United States and the large Ukrainian population in Poland expected this tiny province to become the nucleus of an independent Ukrainian state and to play the role of a Piedmont. The nationalist groups headed by OUN[5] were becoming intensely active in Ruthenia; they were backed in different ways by various German agencies, mainly by those of Rosenberg, Goebbels, the Gestapo, and the army. The international and political activity of pro-German Ukrainian groups was exemplified by the intense propaganda campaign carried on through the radio stations of Vienna, Graz, and Leipzig. The aim of these activities—those of an organizational character in Ruthenia and other important propaganda efforts undertaken abroad—was to promote the concept of an independent Ukrainian state, allied with Germany and cooperating in the realization of German plans in Eastern Europe, with the ultimate goal a unified and independent Great Ukrainian state.

The importance Poland attached to this problem was based on

several contradictory considerations. In the eyes of many influential Poles, Ruthenia was a likely breeding ground for Communist activities, mainly because of its poverty and low level of education. On the other hand, many Poles feared that the German-sponsored propaganda for a Great Ukraine would create in Ruthenia a focus of agitation necessarily affecting the Ukrainians in Poland and thus weakening the Polish state at a time of crucial international tension. Thus, in spite of lively sympathy for the cause of Ukrainian independence, strongly represented in the government, the prevailing opinion was that an independent Ruthenia would bring about difficulties and complications in both domestic and foreign politics.

Polish foreign policy saw a way to eliminate, or at least reduce, these dangers—by Hungary's absorption of Ruthenia, which would re-create the Polish-Hungarian frontier that had existed for centuries. This frontier had contributed to peaceful collaboration throughout the earlier history of both nations and was therefore extremely popular with them. If it could be re-established, it might become part of a broader project—consolidation of the whole Danubian area. With this in mind, Beck had already sought a *rapprochement* between Hungary and Rumania, an effort he believed to be backed by Italy. During his visit to Rome, he and Ciano had agreed to unite Polish and Italian efforts to this end, and thus to oppose indirectly Germany's expansion into the lower Danube area.

But Hitler opposed the proposal that Hungary annex Ruthenia, both during and immediately after Munich. He was not in favor of strengthening ties between mutually friendly nations whose common action might block future German plans. No help was forthcoming from Italy, where, to Ciano's disappointment, Mussolini rejected the idea of a Hungarian-Polish frontier. The strongest opposition was voiced by Rumania, fearful lest Hungary's aggrandizement should encourage her to seek territorial concessions in the formerly Hungarian province of Transylvania. In an effort to reach an agreement on the Hungarian claim to Ruthenia, Beck met King Carol of Rumania on October 19 in Galatz and suggested that Rumania participate by annexing the easternmost tip of Ruthenia. A sizable Rumanian population lived in this area, and the north-south railway line running from Poland would increase transportation facilities between Rumania and Poland, extremely important in any political or military emergency. But Beck failed, for Rumania disagreed with Poland about Czechoslovakia's capabilities. She still believed in the efficacy of the Little Entente system, and desired to maintain her frontier with Czechoslovakia, through which she obtained the products of Czech heavy industry, particularly arms. The Rumanian Government therefore refused to consider a change of policy toward her ally Czechoslovakia.

Apparently Beck was more concerned with the situation south of the Carpathian range—that is, the fate of Slovakia and sub-Carpathian Ruthenia—than he had been with the problem of Teschen, where Poland had a clear and defensible case. He was only too well aware that subservience of rump-Czechoslovakia to German policy would, in the event of a Polish-German conflict, make possible a German strategy of enveloping Poland, the consequences of which—as was to be demonstrated in the campaign of September, 1939—would be disastrous. Then, too, Hungary's possession of Ruthenia would somewhat relieve the pressure of Poland's domestic Ukrainian problem.

Despite her sincere desire for Hungary to obtain sub-Carpathian Ruthenia, Poland was not inclined to give more than advice and diplomatic help. When Count Csaky, at that time *chef de cabinet* to Kanya, the Hungarian Foreign Minister, arrived in Warsaw on October 6, 1938, with Budapest's request that Poland participate in the military occupation of Ruthenia in order to hand it over to Hungary later, Beck firmly refused.[6] He could not find moral justification for even a temporary occupation of a province that had never belonged to Poland. By the end of October, it was evident that Hungarian and Polish efforts to obtain a common frontier would fail. Direct Hungarian-Czechoslovak negotiations about cession of territory to Hungary, initiated in conformity with the Munich agreements, were fruitless. The problem was finally decided by the First Vienna Award. Italy and Germany consigned to Hungary a stretch of territory cut out from Slovakia and Ruthenia, of approximately 5,000 square miles and a population of over a million, the majority of whom were Hungarians. Hungary had to wait several more months for the realization of a common frontier with Poland.

Polish and Soviet interests coincided in the problem of Ruthenia. Moscow, too, was apprehensive about German schemes to stir up Ukrainian nationalism, which could radiate from Ruthenia. This similarity of outlook may have contributed to the period of improved relations between Warsaw and Moscow, inaugurated by the joint communiqué of November 26.[7] This more favorable atmosphere enabled Poland to initiate negotiations with the U.S.S.R. on some long-standing issues. The most important result was a treaty of commerce signed in Moscow on February 19, 1939, and intended to bring about an exchange of goods of up to 100 million zlotys (approximately $20 million). This and other agreements were greeted in Warsaw with satisfaction. But the hope of considerably improved Russo-Polish economic relations was frustrated soon after, when the U.S.S.R. applied the tactics of procrastination that had proved so effective in scuttling the Treaty of Riga concluded nearly twenty years earlier. Polish diplomacy could not foresee the change in Soviet-German relations that was to begin in the spring of 1939. Beck believed no *rapprochement* between the Reich and the U.S.S.R. was possible. Convinced that the ideological abyss between Nazism and Communism could not be bridged, he endeavored to maintain his policy of balancing off Berlin and Moscow. Should Poland's relations with one neighbor seriously deteriorate, he counted on being able, by skillful maneuvering, to re-establish the equilibrium. Such was his intention when he was informed by Lipski of Ribbentrop's "general settlement" proposal of October 24, an unexpected blow presaging grave dangers for Poland.

The contents of the Lipski-Ribbentrop talk were kept secret, not solely at Ribbentrop's request, but because Poland wanted to weigh the significance of the proposal and to avoid premature publicity about the seriousness of her position. Poland's answer was transmitted to Ribbentrop by Lipski on November 19. The interview is recorded in both Polish and German official documents, which show that Lipski read out the instructions received from Beck.[8] The statement rejected the proposed integration of Danzig into the Reich and offered to consider a bilateral Polish-German treaty to replace the League of Nations guarantee. To the question of the highway and railroad across Polish territory, Lipski gave an evasive answer, expressing his belief that a solution would be found. Poland's participation in the anti-Comintern pact was not touched upon. Despite apparent differences, the negotiations were not broken off; both parties continued to study various aspects of their proposals. Germany suspended the negotiations, probably because of Hitler's hesitation over whether to strike first in the east or in the west. Ribbentrop's plans to visit Paris and the negotiations for the Franco-German declaration of December 6 might have been reasons for Germany's relaxing her pressure on Beck for an answer. It was imperative now to avoid any disturbance with France's ally.

But the Germans soon resumed their insistent demands. Beck, on his way back from a vacation on the Riviera, was invited to visit Hitler at Berchtesgaden. The meeting took place on January 5, 1939. Characteristically, Hitler developed the already familiar scheme concerning Danzig, the Corridor, and the anti-Comintern pact. But whereas Ribbentrop had been insistent and had emphatically demanded Danzig's annexation to the Reich and Poland's participation in the anti-Comintern pact, Hitler, being shrewder and more deceptive, did not press these points so strongly; he even assured Beck that there would be no *fait accompli* over Danzig.[9] Beck nevertheless sensed undertones in the conversation, and the next day in Munich he told Ribbentrop that for the first time he was departing with a feeling of pessimism over future Polish-German relations. Yet, despite indications that Germany's attitude toward Poland was becoming more aggressive, these relations remained outwardly unchanged.

At the end of January, Ribbentrop arrived in Warsaw to return Beck's visit of 1935 to Berlin. His presence in the Polish capital on January 26, the fifth anniversary of the signing of the Polish-German declaration, offered an opportunity to emphasize, in official and press communications, the importance and permanence of this agreement. In his conversations with President Moscicki, Marshal Smigly-Rydz, and other officials, Ribbentrop took pains to insist that all pending questions between the two nations could be resolved. But in his private talks with Beck— they met for two hours alone, without witnesses—he again raised the problems previously discussed by him and Hitler with Lipski and Beck, and insisted on positive decisions. Beck answered with candor and explained fully why Poland could not agree to the German proposals. The only question that was settled, and that by a gentleman's agreement, concerned the possibility of withdrawal by the League of Nations of its guarantee of Danzig's constitution. Germany and Poland agreed that in that event they would immediately publish their decision to maintain the *status quo* in Danzig and to negotiate a bilateral agreement. Ribbentrop several times mentioned the Ukrainian problem, alluding to possible compensations for Poland in the Ukraine for concessions on Danzig. Hints about Poland's interests in the Soviet Ukraine, remarks on the common danger to Germany and Poland from the east, allusions to the possibility of joining forces to combat Communism, and finally overt insistence that Poland join the anti-Comintern pact—all indicated clearly that Germany's ultimate aim was to conquer the fertile provinces of central and southern U.S.S.R. Hitler had said to Beck in Berchtesgaden that every Polish division engaged against Russia would be a corresponding saving of a German division. Poland must be drawn into the eastward adventure of Germany, and Hitler was ready to pay a price for such aid—especially since realization of Germany's vast plans would enable him to reclaim it easily. Ribbentrop's offer of a compensation in the Ukraine for concessions on Danzig was a further attempt to lure Poland into a supporting role.

But the Polish Government was determined not to become a satellite of Germany. It intended, as it had clearly asserted, to fulfill strictly the obligations contracted with the U.S.S.R. Thus Poland stood in the way of Germany's advance to the east.

The conversations with Hitler and Ribbentrop had made Beck aware that Polish-German relations were taking a dangerous turn. Thus, it was of utmost importance for Poland to strengthen her ties with the West. The case of Czechoslovakia had demonstrated that an alliance with France alone could be an ineffectual safeguard against German aggression. Besides, it was no secret to Beck that the French Ambassador in Warsaw, Noël, was urging his government to revise the Franco-Polish agreements to eliminate the obligation of immediate assistance.[10] The alliance with France would be of value only if Great Britain were determined to assist Poland in the event of a German attack.

New steps toward a closer collaboration with Great Britain had been taken even before Ribbentrop's visit to Warsaw. Soon after the Munich agreement, the Polish Ambassador in London, Raczynski, had suggested that Beck visit London in connection with the pending meeting of the Committee of Three on Danzig. Beck took up the question with the British Ambassador in Warsaw on January 26, expressing his readiness to go to London. He expected that this visit would give him an opportunity to renew contacts with British political leaders and members of the government. In further talks through diplomatic channels, the first week of April was agreed upon as the most convenient date for the visit, and the scope of subjects to be discussed was enlarged to include the changes in Europe during the last few months as well as a general *tour d'horizon*.[11]

Meanwhile, it was to the interest of neither Poland nor Germany to disclose their failure to reach agreement on the important questions under discussion. Germany still hoped to force decisions on her own terms. Ribbentrop, back from Warsaw, advised Hitler to accelerate the final subjugation of Czechoslovakia in order to demonstrate to the Poles their precarious position.[12] But, for the time being, Germany was endeavoring to appear conciliatory, and this set the tone of Hitler's speech of January 30. He described the relations between Germany and Poland as "one of the reassuring factors in the political life of Europe." This attitude was perplexing since the deterioration in relations was evident from outbreaks of Polish and German students in Danzig followed by retaliatory demonstrations in Warsaw and other Polish cities. German minority leaders in Poland were complaining of discrimination and of only negligible improvement in their situation despite the reciprocal promises of November, 1937.[13] Grievances were also voiced by the Polish minority in Germany. Most especially, the anti-Semitic excesses in Germany and the consequent disgraceful and revolting treatment of Polish Jews who resided in Germany—some of them for many years—aroused a strong wave of resentment in Poland, which found expression in the press and in other reflections of public opinion.[14]

To the annoyance of the government, anti-German street demonstrations occurred in Warsaw during the visit of the Italian Foreign Minister, Ciano, who came to Poland at the end of February to return Beck's visit to Rome. In spite of the friendly relations between Poland and Italy, the result of cultural and historical ties, this visit was not a success. Beck anticipated, on the basis of his discussions with Ciano in Rome, that Italy would support his efforts to achieve stability in the Danube basin through a *rapprochement* between Hungary and Rumania and a common Hungarian-Polish frontier. He received no encouragement. Ciano was reserved, as if attempting to avoid displeasing Germany, and his behavior met with criticism in Poland. No useful purpose was served by the visit.

Quite the opposite was the visit of the new Rumanian Foreign Minister, Gafencu, which took place a few days later. Gafencu made an excellent impression on government and public alike, and complete harmony existed between him and Beck. He abandoned his predecessor's opposition to a common Hungarian-Polish frontier, appreciated Poland's effort to bring about a Hungarian-Rumanian *rapprochement,* and declared himself highly satisfied with his conversations with members of the Polish Government.[15]

This favorable turn, coming at a moment when a wave of optimism was sweeping over Europe because war had been avoided, rendered the Poles more hopeful of the possibility of a betterment in international relations. Within a few days, however, events of great significance shattered this hope. In spite of Prague's efforts to appease him, Hitler decided to effectuate the plan that had been frustrated at Munich by Chamberlain's successful effort to save peace at the cost of Czechoslovakia's territorial integrity. The well-planned dismemberment of post-Munich Czechoslovakia was accomplished by Germany with the usual German ruthlessness.[16]

The Slovaks' dissatisfaction with their degree of autonomy—a dissatisfaction incited and promoted by the usual fifth-column activities—served as a pretext for German intervention in the conflict between Prague and Bratislava. A campaign launched against the Czechs because of atrocities allegedly committed on the German minority in Bohemia and Moravia, accusations of pursuing "a disguised Benes policy," and other charges directed at Prague, preceded the military occupation of Czech lands. President Hacha, who was summoned to Berlin on March 14, agreed to German demands under well-known tragic circumstances. The next day Hitler entered Prague, and the protectorate of Bohemia-Moravia under German rule was proclaimed. A few days later, panic-stricken Slovak leaders signed a treaty with Germany, establishing the latter's almost limitless control over Slovakia. The third part of federal Czechoslovakia, sub-Carpathian Ruthenia, was occupied by Hungary through a previous agreement and with Germany's permission. Meeting no opposition from the local population, the Hungarian troops reached the crest of the Carpathian range and established contact with the Polish frontier guards.

The dismemberment of Czechoslovakia demonstrated to the world that, contrary to expectation, the policy of appeasement had not achieved the peace for which Chamberlain had tried so hard. Faith in Hitler's word was shattered. All his statements and assurances—"the last territorial claim," "the last problem to be solved," and "we don't want any more Czechs"—were now regarded as deceitful phrases and vain promises.[17] Indignation and dismay were general, especially in Great Britain.

Developments on the southern frontier suddenly revealed the seriousness of the German menace to Poland. Hungary's occupation of sub-Carpathian Ruthenia did not compensate for the strategic advantages held by Germany. The wish for a common Hungarian-Polish frontier was realized, but under conditions that did not alleviate Poland's grave concern for security. A few days after the destruction of the Czechoslovak state, Polish security was threatened from the north, too. Hitler demanded the immediate cession of Lithuanian rights to Memel and its reunion with Germany. This surprise demand was made of the Lithuanian Foreign Minister, Urbsys, during a visit to Ribbentrop in Berlin, and had been preceded by the usual agitation of the *Volksgruppe* in Memel. Before the agreement transferring Memel to Germany was even signed, Hitler, in a show of force, sailed along the Polish coast to Memel with a German naval squadron. None of these German actions, which so closely concerned Poland, were announced in advance to the Polish Government—although the day before the signing of the German-Lithuanian treaty annexing Memel to Germany, Lipski had been received by Ribbentrop and had asked about Memel.[18]

Germany's breach of promises to the Western powers and her obvious bad faith brought about a flurry of diplomatic activity, especially by the British Government. For the sake of expediency, the West had permitted the weakening of the League of Nations and of the various arrangements on which collective security might have been built. Now mutual assistance had to be reorganized somehow. Great Britain took the lead. The British Government protested strongly to Berlin the violation of the Munich agreement and the destruction of the Czechoslovak state. Greatly disturbed by rumors of a forthcoming German ultimatum to Rumania, whose territory and resources presented another possible goal of Germany's eastward expansion, the British on March 20 submitted to France, Poland, and the U.S.S.R. a proposal for a four-power declaration that, in the event of a threat to the political independence of any European state, immediate consultations should be held on steps to be taken jointly.[19]

The Polish Government was profoundly alarmed at the rapid succession of events by which Germany had obtained advantages useful in a possible aggressive action against Poland. The treaty of March 22, which forced Lithuania to cede Memel, the treaty of protection between Germany and Slovakia of March 23, and, to a lesser degree, the German-Rumanian trade agreement of the same date aroused the Poles' disapproval of their government's foreign policy and particularly of Beck. But it was not so much the pressure of public opinion as the urgent necessity of checking the German offensive moves against Polish interests that required quick and effective counteraction.

The British proposal for a four-power declaration, indicating a reversal of policy, was a welcome development. But it seemed neither practicable nor acceptable, since collaboration with the U.S.S.R. within the proposed group of states would align Poland with Soviet Russia, destroying the balance so carefully built up and, by offending Germany, increase the danger of war. Also, consultation would not provide the threatened nations with actual security. The Polish Government felt that no commitments should be entered into unless they contained a clear obligation of immediate and automatic assistance in the event of German aggression. The instruction sent by Beck on March 23 to Raczynski, the Polish Ambassador in London—and carried out the next day—told him to inform the British Government of Poland's willingness to consider the proposal further.[20] But it stressed the inevitable complications and delays inherent in multilateral negotiation and suggested to Great Britain a bilateral agreement that could be quickly concluded.

The Polish proposal was favorably received, for the British Government had just obtained information indicating the possibility of an imminent move against Poland by Germany.[21] Following a rapid exchange of views, Chamberlain, who had obtained Poland's agreement, declared in the House of Commons on March 31 that, pending conclusion of consultations then in progress, Great Britain would give Poland all possible support in resisting any action clearly threatening Polish independence.[22] Chamberlain added that he was authorized to announce France's adoption of an identical position. This reassurance by two Western powers was regarded by Warsaw as an important asset in the conversations with Germany.

During the two weeks between the seizure of Czechoslovakia and the announcement of the British guarantee, several other diplomatic initiatives were undertaken in an atmosphere charged with forebodings of imminent aggressive action by Germany. In reaction against the destruction of the Czechoslovak state, a protest was lodged by France, the Soviet Union, and Great Britain against Germany's violation of commitments and of international law. At a Franco-British conference in London, on the occasion of President Lebrun's official visit to England, the tension between Hungary and Rumania—the result of their mobilization in connection with the occupation of sub-Carpathian Ruthenia by Hungary—came up for discussion.[23] Poland endeavored, in collaboration with both Western governments, to exert a moderating influence on Budapest and Bucharest.

The Soviet Union had agreed to the proposal of a four-power declaration, provided that France and Poland would sign it. But Moscow had also brought forward a plan for a six-power conference of France, Great Britain, Poland, Rumania, Turkey, and the U.S.S.R. to be held, preferably in Bucharest, as a demonstration of the common will to oppose the aggression threatening Rumania. This suggestion was considered premature by Great Britain, who preferred to pursue her own plan.

In the midst of all these efforts to organize a mutual-assistance system, to quiet down counterclaims and apprehensions, and to find out which rumors were true, the Polish Government (and particularly the Foreign Minister) was primarily concerned with two problems: first, the negotiations with Great Britain for a mutual-assistance treaty, and second, the decisions to be made in the crisis reached in Polish-German relations after the Lipski-Ribbentrop conversation of March 21.

According to Lipski, Ribbentrop's tone during this conversation "departed considerably from that in which matters affecting the two governments had been previously discussed, and was in the nature of definite pressure."[24] Lipski emphasized Ribbentrop's insistence on the urgency of a Polish decision on Danzig and the highway across the Corridor, and on the proposal for an early meeting between Beck and Hitler, which seemed to indicate that Germany was formulating plans for further rapid expansion eastward; he also noted Ribbentrop's silence about the cession of Memel, which was forced on Lithuania the following day.

Aware of the importance of this conversation, Lipski went to Warsaw to report on it personally. On March 25, Beck gave him instructions, the substance of which was presented to Ribbentrop in writing during their next conversation, on March 26. Poland's reply to Ribbentrop's renewed proposals was conciliatory in form but negative in substance. The Polish Government refused to agree to the incorporation of Danzig into Germany and to an extraterritorial link between East Prussia and the Reich across Polish territory. It suggested, instead, negotiations on increased transit facilities through Polish Pomerania and on the status of Danzig.[25]

Ribbentrop, whose attitude Lipski described as "distinctly cool," did not see a basis for a settlement in the Polish reply. In his opinion, the relations between the two countries were rapidly deteriorating. The next day, he sent for Lipski again and complained about alleged excesses against the German minority in Poland and about hostile demonstrations against Germany. This phase of the conversations was concluded in Warsaw on March 28, by Beck and Ambassador von Moltke. Referring to Ribbentrop's statement that Polish aggression in Danzig would be regarded as directed at Germany itself, Beck informed the German Ambassador that any German intervention to change Danzig's status would be considered an aggression against Poland.[26]

Despite their increasingly menacing attitude toward the Poles, the Germans did not then intend to provoke Poland into action, fearing that they would drive her into Great Britain's arms. Hitler's long-range plans were to defeat Poland so completely as to deprive her of any political importance, and to shift Germany's eastern frontier deep into Polish lands. But for the moment the Poles were not to be aroused. Hitler was sure he could wear them down and make them yield to his demands. Entirely misjudging the Polish attitude, he even considered it possible that the Polish Government would be unable to take responsibility for the cession of Danzig and would tacitly welcome military occupation of the Free City by the Germans.[27] For the time being, German diplomatic missions abroad were instructed to avoid discussion of the German-Polish problem.

In this atmosphere of suspense and rising tension, Beck left for London, as had been arranged, on April 3. He was authorized by President Moscicki and Marshal Smigly-Rydz to offer the British Government a reciprocal commitment converting the British unilateral guarantee into an actual alliance. Poland's obligations, however, had to remain secret for the time being.[28] But Beck's favorable evaluation of Britain's attitude toward Poland induced him to make public the mutual-assistance pledge. His conversations with Chamberlain and Halifax had persuaded him that Great Britain was determined to employ force, if necessary, to oppose Hitler's further aggressions. He was convinced that the Germans, "who had lost the notion of responsibility,"[29] could be stopped in their plans of blackmail only by a strong show of opposition, and that only thus might peace yet be saved.

The outline of the future Anglo-Polish treaty, as well as the points to be settled by further negotiations, were laid down in a summary of conclusions[30] approved and initialed by Halifax and Beck. A communiqué summed up the conversations. It was so drafted that in case of urgency it could be converted into the agreement itself. In fact, though not yet in form, Beck's negotiations in London resulted in an Anglo-Polish alliance. The way of neutrality was closed to each of them in the event of a German attack on the other. The specter of a two-front war, which the Germans dreaded and which Hitler had been endeavoring to avoid, was thus revived.

Beck was aware of the risk involved in Poland's momentous decision to join forces with Great Britain. He tried to minimize its effect on the Germans by interpreting it as a mere extension of the Franco-Polish alliance, already accepted by the German Government at the time of the signing of the nonaggression declaration of January, 1934. This interpretation was given by Lipski to Weizsäcker on April 6. The Polish Ambassador stressed the bilateral and defensive character of the Anglo-Polish commitments and Poland's refusal to join any anti-German bloc of states. But Weizsäcker rejected this interpretation. In effect, he announced the withdrawal of Hitler's "magnanimous" offer of a global solution and turned down the Polish proposals of March 26.[31] Neither Beck nor Lipski knew at that time that Hitler had already decided to attack Poland. On April 3, the day of Beck's arrival in London, a top-secret directive on preparations for the war with Poland was given out by the German high command under the code name of

"Operation White." Hitler had appended to it the order that "Plans for this operation have to be completed so that it can be carried through at any time from 1.9.1939 [September 1, 1939], onward."[32] Further directives issued April 11 charged political leaders with confining the war to Poland. Hitler's reaction to the Anglo-Polish agreement was limitless wrath and fury.[33]

During the three days of conversations between Beck and the British statesmen, agreement was reached on several questions outside the main mutual-assistance treaty. Other problems were left for further consideration. Great Britain persisted in her intention to draw the U.S.S.R. into the "peace front" that she was building in collaboration with France.[34] Poland in no way opposed these efforts, but she was not willing to join in them and persistently refused to become aligned with the Soviet Union. Beck was convinced that doing so would immediately bring on war with Germany. He reserved his opinion about including Rumania in the proposed system, pending consultation with the allied Rumanian Government. He did not want to lose the opportunity to influence Hungarian policy by a precipitate decision on extending the Polish-Rumanian alliance to cover an attack from the west.

Poland's position in the Rumanian problem was resolved soon after Beck's return from London. In mid-April, the Rumanian Foreign Minister, Gafencu, passed through Poland on his way to Western Europe. Beck took this opportunity to meet him and to clarify the essential points of mutual Polish-Rumanian obligations. The two ministers agreed that the Polish-Rumanian alliance had established a general obligation of mutual aid. Technical arrangements covered only the event of Soviet aggression, but in an emergency additional agreements could be rapidly negotiated to extend the obligation to cover German or Hungarian aggression. It was understood that Rumania was strong enough to resist Hungary alone, but should Germany join Hungary in a thrust against Rumania, Poland would bear the brunt of the attack anyway, and thus give full help to her ally. On Beck's request, Gafencu reported their agreement to the British statesmen when he, in turn, visited London on April 23.

Fear of further international complications grew rapidly. On

Good Friday, April 7, Italy invaded Albania. Concern for the *status quo* established in the Mediterranean area by the Italo-British agreements of April 16 and November 16, 1938, aroused British and French efforts to support the nations threatened by expansion of the Axis powers into the Balkans, and quickened their endeavors to complete plans for a wide system of collective security. Greece and Yugoslavia seemed to be most vulnerable to attack. The Yugoslav Government, taking into consideration its improved relations with Italy, the dangers it would be exposed to in case of friction with Germany, and its own domestic situation, refused the Western guarantee. Greece, alarmed at rumors that Italy intended to occupy Corfu, accepted the British offer. Chamberlain, in a speech in the House of Commons on April 13, extended the British guarantee to Greece and, on French insistence but with some misgivings, to Rumania.[35] On the same day, Daladier issued a statement to the press in which he broadened France's obligations in the Balkan peninsula to cover Greece and Rumania. He expressed satisfaction with the Anglo-Polish agreement, and confirmed the alliance between France and Poland, an alliance mutually guaranteeing each other "immediately and directly" against any menace to their vital interests.

The Anglo-French guarantees were received in Greece and Rumania with great satisfaction by the people but "with a mixture of gratitude and embarrassment" by their governments, which endeavored to minimize their significance in the eyes of the Italian and German leaders.[36] Nevertheless, the Anglo-French declarations, followed by Roosevelt's message of April 14 to Hitler and Mussolini,[37] increased hope in the possibility of avoiding war. These declarations created a very favorable reaction in Poland. But Beck remained skeptical about an alliance of Southeastern European states, which he thought might prove as ineffectual as had the Little Entente system in the case of Czechoslovakia.

Hitler's speech in the Reichstag revealed the extent of his resentment at the endeavors to organize a collective defense against German expansionism.[38] The speech was a vindication of Germany's violations of the Munich agreements, based on Hitler's singular conception of justice and right. He repudiated the Anglo-

German naval convention and the Polish-German declaration of nonaggression, arguing that Great Britain and Poland had unilaterally nullified those agreements by their encirclement policy. He listed his "unrenewable" offers made to Poland for her agreement to German annexation of Danzig and the granting of an extraterritorial highway and railroad across the Corridor. In his usual manner, he adapted the facts to the needs of his presentation. Finally he ridiculed Roosevelt's solemn appeal to him for a ten years' truce. Expertly written memoranda, summing up Hitler's arguments on the German-Polish and Anglo-German problems, were delivered on the same day to the Polish Ministry of Foreign Affairs and to the British Foreign Office, respectively. The speech as well as the memoranda theoretically left the way open for a peaceful solution of the controversial questions. The British Ambassador, Henderson, quite rightly interpreted these moves as intended to represent Germany later as the injured party whose offers had been rejected.[39]

Beck's answer to Hitler, given in a speech in Parliament on May 5, won unanimous approval in Poland and was praised by the British and French. Beck spoke with studious moderation. He corrected several of Hitler's misleading statements alluding vaguely to German proposals of a joint thrust against the Soviet Union, and concluded by stating that Poland was ready to negotiate under conditions of equality in order to re-establish neighborly relations with Germany. A memorandum, courteous and conciliatory in form, developing the legal and diplomatic arguments used by Beck in his speech, was delivered by the Polish Embassy to the German Foreign Ministry.[40]

These two spectacular pronouncements—Hitler's speech and Beck's answer—were followed by a stalemate. This confirmed Lipski's pessimistic estimate of the situation and induced him to tender his resignation. He reasoned that since he was the one who had signed the 1934 declaration, he could hardly expect, under reversed conditions in Germany, that his further efforts could produce any useful results. Though Beck did not deny Lipski's arguments, he asked him to carry on at least temporarily as Ambassador in Berlin.[41] The Polish Foreign Minister, sharing the opinion of the British Government, believed that Polish-German negotiations were still possible. But the Germans did not intend to resume them. Von Moltke left for Germany without waiting for Beck to return from London and, when he came back to Warsaw, made no attempt to establish contact with the Foreign Minister.

Germany's objective now was to isolate Poland, discredit her, and wear her down in order to provoke dissension and disunity in the opposite camp, and, at the same time, to consolidate Germany's international position and stimulate military preparation. The Pact of Steel, signed May 22, was calculated to impress world opinion and to draw Italy more closely into German plans. The military preparation included the completion of the West Wall, a line of fortifications along Germany's western border, the increase of armored, motorized, and airborne forces, and the expansion of the navy and the air force.

The continuous and gigantic growth of the German armed forces, and the shift of German industry to war production, were observed with anxiety by Poland and her Western allies. The display of German might in connection with the occupation of Prague and Memel, as well as certain subterfuges used in Danzig to facilitate the organization of a disguised army and to smuggle men and arms from East Prussia, indicated that rumors about a coup in Danzig through a staged internal revolt might well be justified. These circumstances demanded at least a partial mobilization of Polish forces, and accordingly four infantry divisions, one cavalry brigade, and certain classes of specialists were called up. The Polish general staff intensified its studies of German strategy and began to perfect defense and fortification plans.

These measures soon became heavy burdens for Polish finances.[42] The necessity of expanding industrial production and acquiring military equipment abroad confronted the Polish Government with additional problems. An internal loan was being subscribed with patriotic enthusiasm but at the cost of taking the limited funds thus obtained out of the national economy. Still, stocks of raw materials had to be replenished by purchases abroad, and it was feared that without foreign credit these expenditures would weaken the national currency. The Polish Government hoped that the West, particularly Great Britain, having backed Poland politically, would grant her financial assistance for improving her war potential.

Beck had refused to include economic matters in the agenda of his London talks, not wishing to combine political and commercial problems. Once back in Warsaw, he spoke tentatively to the British Ambassador, Sir Howard Kennard, about Poland's need for financial support, and instructed Raczynski to follow up with Chamberlain and Halifax.[43] In principle, the British Government reacted favorably. A Polish delegation, headed by the governor of the Bank of Poland, Adam Koc, left in June for London.

From the very start of the negotiations, a considerable discrepancy separated Polish hopes and British offers. The basic approaches were different. The Polish Government had in mind a long-range financial and economic adjustment; the Treasury and the Bank of England were mainly interested in helping Poland purchase arms, which Great Britain herself needed and could supply in limited quantities only. The Poles wanted commercial credits and a cash loan in free currency. The British were willing to grant export credits for the purchase of munitions within the Commonwealth, but they attached to the grant of a cash loan convertible in bullion or foreign exchange conditions that seemed too onerous to the Poles.[44] Instead of the £50 million or at least £25 million requested, the British Government offered approximately 8 million in export credits and 5.5 million in transferable cash loans. In spite of mutual efforts to bridge the gap, only the commercial credit of over 8 million was agreed upon in July. Simultaneously, a parallel French credit of 430 million francs was acquired. Cash credits were not granted by Great Britain until September 7—six days after the invasion of Poland had actually begun. War matériel purchased in England was shipped too late to reach Poland before the war started.

The leisurely course of these financial negotiations and their virtual failure had grave consequences for Poland. Because of inadequate financial support, the Polish Army's equipment needs could not be satisfied; the result was that Poland's considerable human resources were not drawn upon sufficiently when war broke out. Abroad, especially in Germany, the breakdown of financial negotiations was interpreted as proof that effective Anglo-French assistance to Poland need not be feared.[45]

Inasmuch as financial matters were discussed mainly with Great Britain, military questions had to be settled primarily between Warsaw and Paris. Daladier's declaration of April 13, confirming the full validity of the Franco-Polish alliance, made detailed staff agreements an urgent matter. In preparation for them, Lukasiewicz, Polish Ambassador in Paris, negotiated with Foreign Minister Bonnet an agreement aimed at adjusting the stipulations of alliance to the situation created by the Anglo-Polish arrangements of April 6. The Franco-Polish military convention was interpreted in this document as implying reciprocal, immediate (*sur-le-champs*), and direct assistance in the event of aggression. In an appendix, Poland qualified the problem of Danzig as vital to her, and France acknowledged this declaration. Thus an attack on Danzig would bring into play the *casus foederis*. On May 12, the French cabinet unanimously confirmed the text of a political protocol in accordance with the Bonnet-Lukasiewicz agreement.[46] The same day, General Kasprzycki, Minister of Military Affairs of Poland, left Warsaw for Paris in order to complete this interpretive protocol by precise understandings and coordination of strategy between the two armies. His counterpart in the general-staff conversations was General Gamelin, chief of the general staff, commander in chief in time of war. In his memoirs,[47] Gamelin admits having been dissatisfied with Kasprzycki's arrival, because he felt that Franco-Soviet talks should precede concrete negotiations with the Polish Army. Hence, in his talks with Kasprzycki, he endeavored to avoid precision and to introduce a flexible interpretation of the concept of military assistance. He disliked the spontaneous promise, made to the Poles by General Vuillemin, chief of the French air force, to act vigorously in their support in the event of German aggression, as well as the similar declarations of General Georges, commander of the northern sector of the French Army, concerning operations on his sector of the front.[48] The record of the conversations, in the form of a secret document, containing reciprocal assurances of action to be taken by both armies in common defense against a German attack, was signed on May 19. But Gamelin, after consultation with the Quai d'Orsay, attached to it a letter by which he made the military agreement dependent on the signing of the political protocol. Bonnet, on his return from Geneva, where he had discussed with Halifax Anglo-Franco-Polish problems, delayed signing the protocol and later set it aside.[49] Gamelin consequently regarded as not binding the document he had signed with Kasprzycki and the measures they had determined. The Poles believed that assurances given by responsible quarters in conformity with vital interests of both countries could not be disavowed. They expected French support against a German attack to the extent of the verbal and written promises given Kasprzycki in Paris. Gamelin withheld his interpretation from them lest they might be discouraged in opposing German aggression. These differences were responsible for a lack of adjustment and coordination in strategic plans between the two allied armies, which were soon to be engaged in a deadly struggle with a technically superior enemy.

Great Britain's decision to rely upon Poland and her army to resist the German attack until Western and—it was hoped—Soviet forces were ready for action implied another round of staff conversations, this time between Polish and British military leaders.

Since Poland expected no direct help from British armed forces, except possibly naval and air support, the talks were mainly a very complete exchange of information on all political and strategic problems of interest to the two armies. These talks were conducted in Warsaw to give British experts a firsthand view of the structure and plans of the Polish Army. During the last week in May, a small group of officers, headed by General Clayton, Commander Rawlings, and Air Force Colonel Davidson, met with General Stachiewicz, Polish chief of staff. In July, General Ironside, chief of the imperial general staff, spent several days in Poland conferring with Marshal Smigly-Rydz and other military commanders. He was also received by President Moscicki, and met Beck and other members of the government.[50] The most important matter, according to the Polish Army's viewpoint, was the action that the British air force would undertake in support of Poland. The Poles were convinced that at the outbreak of the war the whole might of Germany's land, naval, and air forces would be directed against them. Their own limited air force was sufficient for no more than defensive and protective action. Hence they felt that attacks on German military objectives should be undertaken by the British air force. This was virtually promised by General Clayton, and later confirmed by General Ironside, who foresaw that more detailed arrangements would have to be made by British and Polish military experts.

The hope of obtaining British help in keeping Poland's sea communications open could not be fulfilled. It was clearly stated that the British Navy's primary task was to safeguard the main imperial communication lines. This implied that the Germans would be able to cut off and control the Baltic Sea from the very start of the war. Therefore the small Polish Navy would have to be sent out of the Baltic as soon as war broke out.

Unfortunately the Warsaw conversations with the British generals were not followed by more precise arrangements. The Poles, who maintained an attitude of calm and confidence, did not exert pressure on their allies for definite plans of action. They were guilty of excessive trust in general assurances of support from the Western allies, and of overconfidence in their own preparedness. The British statesmen hoped that by stressing repeatedly and insistently their determination to fulfill the terms of their guarantee to Poland, they would induce Germany to solve controversial questions by peaceful means. They knew that if Hitler applied force, Poland would resist aggression, but that Great Britain could hardly give fighting reality to its guarantees. Consequently they persevered in efforts to extend the "peace front." The British Government believed that the cooperation of the Soviet Union might well become a decisive factor either in maintaining peace or, in case of war, in the successful defense of the attacked countries. With patience and perseverance they pursued endeavors to include the Soviet Union in the coalition against aggression.

Despite Moscow's repeated assurances that Litvinov's dismissal on May 3 and his replacement by Molotov in no way meant a change of U.S.S.R. foreign policy, a reversal of policy was in fact taking shape. Significantly, the usual German attacks and diatribes against the Soviet Union were discontinued at this time. It is now known that secret conversations between Berlin and Moscow had been going on since April, 1939; but at that time world public opinion attached little weight to the rumors concerning a change in Russo-German relations. It was assumed that the ideological chasm between Communism and Nazism was an insuperable obstacle to a Berlin-Moscow collaboration. Since May, however, isolated reports and information on this change of policy had begun to reach the Western governments. Washington was the best informed. The State Department regularly obtained secret information on the German-Soviet talks, which started as economic conversations in January, and, after interruption, were resumed on April 17 in a conversation between the Soviet Ambassador in Berlin, Merekalov, and Weizsäcker.[51] From the start of May, the American Embassy in Moscow supplied Washington with current information on these negotiations, which were still being conducted in great secrecy. They dragged on, for both sides had specific reasons for hesitation and delay. The Germans had to take into account the reactions of their partners in the anti-Comintern pact, especially Japan, and the Russians were playing for time in order to use their negotiations with Great Britain and France to obtain a better bargain from the Germans. Finally, at the beginning of August, a marked improvement in relations between Berlin and Moscow led to Soviet-German discussions of political problems. Talks between German Ambassador Schulenburg and Molotov resulted, on August 19, in the conclusion of a mutually advantageous trade and credit agreement. Two days later, Berlin announced that the commercial agreement would be followed shortly by a nonaggression pact with the Soviet Union, and on August 22, Ribbentrop's visit to Moscow was revealed by the official Soviet news agency, Tass.

It is remarkable that information on the Soviet-German secret negotiations was so scarce, and that that which reached the West did not find more belief and rouse more attention. As early as May 7, the French Government had a confidential report from Ambassador Coulondre on the probability of Soviet-German collusion.[52] Apparently the Quai d'Orsay attached little importance to this, for there is no indication that the report was passed on to the British and Polish governments. Nor does it appear that the U.S. used its valuable information to warn and advise its potential allies of the turn in Soviet-German relations. From May to August 22, the Western powers, unwilling to believe that there had been a reversal in Moscow's policy, continued to negotiate with the U.S.S.R. In spite of difficulties and Moscow's delaying tactics, the conversations seemed to be leading to an Anglo-French-Soviet coalition. Poland was kept informed of every phase of the negotiations; but the Polish Government maintained its original aloof attitude and expressed its opinion only when consulted. On May 14, in an instruction to diplomatic missions, Beck summed up the reasons for this attitude, and emphasized that Polish participation in a mutual-assistance treaty with the Soviet Union would be certain to provoke a German attack and start a world conflict.[53] He had little faith in the success of these Anglo-French-Soviet negotiations, but they confirmed his opinion that rumors of a Soviet-German *rapprochement* were without foundation.[54] His conversations, on May 10, with Potemkin, the Deputy Commissar for Foreign Affairs, supported his conviction that such a *rapprochement* was impossible. Potemkin, stopping in Warsaw after a tour of the Balkan capitals, unhesitatingly assured Beck that in the event of an armed conflict with Germany, Poland could count on the benevolent attitude of the U.S.S.R.[55]

A conversation between the Polish Ambassador in Moscow, Grzybowski, and Molotov, on May 7, 1939, strengthened Beck's feeling that it would be against Polish interests to participate in the negotiations with the Soviets. Molotov revealed to Grzybowski, in an apparently frank and not unfriendly manner, the conditions under which the Soviet Union would sign the agreement with Great Britain and France. Those that concerned Poland were the right of Soviet troops to pass through Polish territory, the dissolution of the Polish alliance with Rumania, and the limitation of British guarantees to Poland's western frontiers only.[56]

The Poles, although aware of the importance of Soviet assistance in the event of war with Germany, could not accept conditions so obviously menacing to Poland's freedom of action and territorial integrity. Poland's misgivings and apprehensions were shared by the Rumanian Government, now faced with similar demands from Moscow. Poland and Rumania interfered with British efforts because of their distrust of Moscow's intentions, their skepticism as to what support would be obtainable from the Soviets in the event of war, and their fear of provoking Hitler. England was trying to construct a mutual-assistance system including Moscow, Paris, and London that would guarantee the smaller nations willing to resist German aggression. Yet the states "threatened with support" began to oppose these generous but (because of the U.S.S.R.) dangerous endeavors of the British Government. Their reasoning is best expressed in a statement made by a Rumanian delegate to the League of Nations in a conversation with Halifax: ". . . public opinion would be disturbed if there should be any suggestion that the only way to escape German aggression was to be occupied by the Soviet Union." [57]

The western neighbors of Russia rightly concluded that in the tripartite agreement Moscow aspired to play the role of main partner in the east, to whose interests the smaller participants in the system—Poland, Rumania, and the Baltic states—would entirely subordinate theirs. Actually, the Soviet Union herself did not need additional security, since her western borders were safeguarded by the Anglo-French guarantees to Poland and Rumania. Invoked, these guarantees would oppose German aggression right at the eastern frontier of Germany, well before any threat to Soviet territory. Thus it is most probable that Moscow negotiated with the Western powers only to obtain the legal right to subordinate her smaller neighbors if the time came when she would be in a position to do so.

The course of these negotiations was protracted and wearisome, characterized by illusory progress and recurring setbacks. The British Government, taking the lead, gradually acceded to all Russian demands on the principles, the scope, and the functioning of the mutual-support agreement. Almost word for word, Molotov's wishes, suggestions, and claims appeared in successive drafts. [58]

Poland became involved in the last stage of the negotiations in

mid-August, when a Franco-British military mission, headed by
General Doumenc and Admiral Drax, arrived in Moscow and
Marshal Voroshilov, chairman of the U.S.S.R. delegation, raised
the question of the Soviet Army's right to pass through Polish and
Rumanian territory and indicated the gates of Vilna and Lwów
as the routes in Poland.[59] France and Great Britain undertook to
negotiate the matter with Warsaw.

The Polish Government, distrustful of Soviet *bona fides* and sus-
pecting ulterior motives, refused. The French, in search of a solution, decided to override the Polish objection, which was, in their
opinion, based on undue suspicion. General Doumenc was authorized by the French Government to give Voroshilov an "affirmative
answer," and he did so on the evening of August 22. But in the
meantime the Soviet reversal of policy had been disclosed by the
announcement of Ribbentrop's imminent arrival in Moscow to
sign the Soviet-German treaty. Voroshilov refused to convene a
meeting of the military conference, expressed dissatisfaction with
Doumenc's declaration, and requested direct affirmation by Poland and Rumania of their agreement to his demand.

To counteract the impact of Soviet-German collaboration, the
French and British governments renewed their pressure on Warsaw. Beck, who appreciated the motives of the Western allies,
agreed on August 23 to authorize Doumenc to make the following
statement in Moscow: "We have learned for certain that in the
event of common action against German aggression, collaboration,
under technical conditions to be settled subsequently between
Poland and the U.S.S.R., is not excluded."[60]

The inference was that after war had actually broken out, a
modification of the Polish attitude could be expected. The French
Government interpreted Beck's agreement to this statement as a
substantial concession that should satisfy the Soviet Government.
But Moscow was not interested in resuming political or military
conversations with the West. The Russians, having played both
sides, now chose the one that promised them the most immediate
advantages. The Ribbentrop-Molotov pact and its secret protocol
fulfilled Soviet desires that the Western powers could not satisfy.

The French and British ambassadors called on Molotov on August 25 and, on instructions from their governments, asked him about the Soviet Government's intentions in the negotiations. Molotov answered—as Voroshilov had done earlier in the day to the military delegations of France and Great Britain—that in the changed political situation the negotiations could not be continued.

Until the very last moment, Stalin and Molotov had concealed their intention of reversing Soviet policy. Their skillful maneuvering had made it difficult for the French and British negotiators to comprehend the real intentions of the U.S.S.R. For the Western diplomats, their laborious efforts in their lengthy and complicated discussions with the Russians were a humiliating experience.

Germany's war of nerves on Poland was not the least motive for the Western powers' eagerness to arrive at an understanding with the Soviet Union before some inadvertent incident precipitated hostilities. It had started in May, immediately after the exchange of speeches by Hitler and Beck, and it continued with varying intensity until the end of August.[61] German propaganda, made up of groundless accusations and derogatory insinuations directed at Poland, obviously aimed either at breaking down the Poles' resistance and forcing them to accede to Hitler's demands, or at provoking them into some action that would enable Germany to brand Poland an aggressor. Either result would achieve Hitler's main objective, for it would nullify the mutual-support agreements between Poland and the Western powers, thus enabling him to deal with the Poles alone.

Between May and August, the tension continued to mount. Poland and Great Britain cooperated fully, with frequent and detailed consultations on Danzig and related questions. In spite of the eagerness of the British Government to bring about negotiations between Poland and Germany, Great Britain understood the importance to Poland of her rights in the Free City. In the course of his London talks, Beck had declared that he would regard Germany's seizure of Danzig or the Corridor as a direct threat to Poland's independence and integrity, and the British Government had accepted this view. Beck was eager to keep the British leaders informed and to consult them on any development requiring common action, but the British Embassy constantly asked for Polish reactions to purely hypothetical events. Beck and his associates could hardly give a precise opinion on what would happen if, say, Danzig suddenly declared its union with Germany. Nevertheless, they were always willing to discuss with their allies any new development that bore on the whole situation.

Great Britain was understandably concerned that a *coup* might precipitate Polish intervention and thus the war that Great Britain was anxious to avoid. In Danzig, the signs of militarization and preparations for a *coup* were unmistakable. The number of incidents multiplied toward the end of June. Great Britain and France decided then to set forth what their position would be in the event of a violent change in the status of the Free City. On July 1, Bonnet sent a note to Ribbentrop emphasizing that France stood ready to assist Poland if she resisted a modification of the Danzig *status quo*. Chamberlain, speaking in Commons, stated that Great Britain was firmly resolved to take similar steps.[62] But, at the same time, the British Government insisted in Warsaw that precautions must be taken to avoid incidents and anti-German disturbances that might spark an open outbreak of hostilities between Poland and Germany.

On its own initiative, the Polish Government made special efforts to avoid incidents between the Polish authorities or population and the German minority. Beck dispatched high-ranking officials of the Ministry of Foreign Affairs to the western provinces to alert local authorities to the danger in any action that German propaganda might brand provocative. The most explosive point of contact was, of course, Danzig. There the bold activities of the Nazi Party and the members of the administration could at any moment force Poland to apply strong measures to defend her rights. Arms were smuggled across the border into Danzig, mostly from East Prussia, and were even brought in at night by air. The local SA and SS organizations were reinforced with large numbers of "tourists." The fact that Polish officials and guards supervised the customs offices greatly hampered these illegal activities. Thus the Nazis tended to demand removal of the control system established by Polish-Danzig agreements and League of Nations decisions, and to create conditions that would make it impossible for Polish customs officials to control the smuggling of men and arms. Several incidents between May and July were the result of these endeavors. The most serious was an attack on May 21 on the customs station at Kalthof on the East Prussian border. The station was demolished by a mob led by uniformed Nazis. Other incidents even resulted in casualties on both sides.

The incidents reached their peak in August. On August 4, Polish customs officials were informed by Danzig authorities that, from August 6 on, they would not be allowed to perform their duties. This was a clear infringement of Polish rights, and it brought a time-limited note from the Polish Commissioner General demanding withdrawal of the order. The Danzig authorities denied that such a measure had been taken, although written proof of it existed.[63] A few days later Weizsäcker summoned the Polish Chargé d'Affaires in Berlin and read him a strongly worded protest against the "ultimatum" to Danzig. Properly, Germany had no right to intervene in relations between Poland and Danzig. The Polish Government therefore expressed its surprise at this protest, in a statement read to the German Chargé d'Affaires in Warsaw by the Undersecretary of State, who repeated Beck's April declaration to Von Moltke that any German interference in Poland's relations with Danzig would be considered an act of aggression. After that, the incident seemed to be closed, but commentaries in the Western press, interpreting it as a backdown by Danzig, aroused a strong reaction in Germany.

Parallel to the increasing war of nerves against Poland were Germany's surreptitious maneuvers to disrupt the antiaggression front and to separate the Poles from their Western allies. To this end a Swedish industrialist, Birger Dahlerus, organized a secret meeting of his friend Goering with a group of prominent British businessmen on August 10. On this occasion, Goering repeated Hitler's assurance that Danzig and the Corridor were Germany's last territorial claims.[64] A similar diversion was Hitler's conversation with the League High Commissioner in Danzig, Burckhardt, in which Hitler proclaimed his desire for peace and close cooperation with Great Britain.[65] All these attempts were useless, for the continuous frank exchange of information between Warsaw and London, facilitated by Ambassador Kennard's friendly but objective reporting to his government, contributed to foiling Germany's intrigue. Relations between Poland and Great Britain improved steadily.

In this dangerous situation, the Polish Government expressed to Halifax its desire to conclude the mutual assistance treaty as soon as possible, and on August 17 submitted a draft to him. The text was easily completed within a few days. However, the news of Ribbentrop's visit to Moscow gave Great Britain a brief moment of indecision—a pessimistic reaction that suggested the possibility of seeking another compromise. But Polish insistence that only a strong demonstration of solidarity could overcome the momentary setback of the allies persuaded the British Government to sign the treaty forthwith.

The "Agreement between the Government of the United Kingdom and the Polish Government regarding Mutual Assistance," signed on August 25, provided for mutual support in the event of direct or indirect aggression by a European power against either country; the decision as to the *casus foederis* was to be made in full consultation.[66] A secret protocol limited the definition of "European power" to Germany and listed the danger areas in which the two governments had particular interests.[67] It also included a clause, clearly aimed at the Soviet Union, that neither government would enter into an agreement with a third party that would prejudice the independence and territorial inviolability of the other.

Warsaw was greatly satisfied with this treaty, one of the most important achievements of Polish foreign policy. It helped offset the Moscow-Berlin agreement. It ruled out any successful German maneuvers to separate the Western powers from Poland. In signing it, Great Britain pledged the full power of the British Empire in defense of Poland's territorial integrity and political independence. For her part, Poland attested that, given the choice between collaboration with totalitarian Germany and solidarity with the West, she would unhesitatingly join with the Western democracies in defending Europe's freedom.

The Anglo-Polish treaty took Hitler by surprise. He had expected that the Soviet-German agreement would change the attitude of the Western powers, discouraging Great Britain and France from assisting Poland. Since this had failed, he now made one more effort to drive a wedge between Poland and her Western allies. He summoned the British Ambassador, Sir Nevile Henderson, and made him a comprehensive offer. In return for British withdrawal from Polish-German problems, he proposed an agreement on the most important questions—colonies and disarmament—and offered a German guarantee of the British Empire. He asked Henderson to fly to London with this proposal, which the latter did on August 26. In a conversation with the French Ambassador, Coulondre, Hitler emphasized the needlessness of a Franco-German war, and asked him to convey to Daladier his feeling of pain at the thought of fighting the French.[68]

Hitler's haste and urgency in speaking to the two ambassadors was understandable: He had already ordered German commanders to invade Poland at dawn the next day, August 26. However, the afternoon of the twenty-fifth, Berlin got news of the signing of the Anglo-Polish treaty and of Mussolini's announcement that he was not ready to enter a war on Germany's side. These developments prompted Hitler to countermand the attack on Poland.[69] He ordered his military commanders "to stop everything at once," and informed Goering, in command of the air force, that he needed time to negotiate—that is, to attempt to eliminate British intervention.

Preparations to invade Poland were so far advanced that in at least two instances the revocation of orders did not arrive in time: German infantry from Slovakian territory attacked the Jablonkow pass in the Carpathian Mountains and secret police occupied the Polish Consulate in Kwidzyn (German: Marienwerder) in East Prussia. In both cases, embarrassed apologies were offered to Polish authorities. From the disquieting troop movements all along the Polish-German border, it could be inferred that the decision to strike had not been abandoned but merely delayed.

The most sensitive point was clearly Danzig. An elaborate program of provocations and gradual curtailment of Poland's rights was being effected by the Danzig administration, with advice and help from Edmund Veesenmayer, prominent Nazi and special representative of Ribbentrop.[70] Reprisals were planned against Poles for alleged accumulations of arms planted by Germans. Instead of an announced courtesy visit by the cruiser "Königsberg," the German Government sent to Danzig on August 25 the battleship "Schleswig-Holstein." She did not leave when she was supposed to, but lay moored near the "Westerplatte." The Polish naval installations on the Hel peninsula were within easy range of her 11-inch guns.[71] On August 24, the Senate of Danzig, in gross violation of the Constitution, appointed the Nazi *Gauleiter* Forster as head of state. Since Danzig's Constitution was guaranteed by the League of Nations, it was not Poland alone but the League, or the great powers in its name, that were responsible for defending it. Nevertheless, the Polish Government addressed a strong protest to the Senate. The League's High Commissioner, Burckhardt, also raised objections to Forster's appointment, but without results. Meanwhile, Polish rights in Danzig were drastically violated, stocks of merchandise were confiscated, control of the railways was taken over by Danzig, and Poles—even members of a negotiating team—were put under arrest. According to a report of the French Consul, all these measures combined to convert the Free City into an entrenched camp.[72] But the gravity of the international situation and the determination to avoid steps that could aggravate the tension rendered inadvisable anything stronger than remonstrances and protests.

Beck took an extremely serious view of the events in Danzig. He agreed with the British suggestions that an effort should be undertaken to relieve the tension. He therefore instructed Lipski to seek an interview with Weizsäcker to clarify the points at issue. Weizsäcker being unavailable, Lipski took advantage of an incidental invitation of Goering to call on him. The meeting took place on August 24. The conversation, friendly in tone, concluded with Goering's statement that the Danzig question and other controversies would not have reached the critical stage were it not for the British-Polish alliance. He repeatedly insinuated that Great Britain would give Poland no help at all.[73]

Goering's argument was clearly another maneuver to separate

Poland from her Western allies. With the same intent he again put to work his Swedish friend Dahlerus, who traveled back and forth between Berlin and London; in personal interviews with Chamberlain and Halifax, Dahlerus endeavored to persuade the British Government of Germany's sincere wish to reach an agreement. But his ignorance of politics and his naïve acceptance of German allegations finally caused the London Foreign Office to refuse to listen to him. An interesting and little-known episode of Dahlerus' activity was the plan for Goering's secret journey to London, which came very close to being realized.[74]

Dahlerus' secret mission, conducted simultaneously with the official Anglo-German negotiations, did not change the British Government's attitude. Henderson, back from London, was received by Hitler on August 28. The British cabinet's answer to Hitler's offer was that it would not, for any advantage, agree to a settlement that would jeopardize Poland's independence. It proposed direct Polish-German negotiations and an international guarantee of the resulting agreement. Only after the settlement of differences between Germany and Poland could negotiations on larger issues between London and Berlin take place.[75] In fact, Great Britain assumed the role of a mediator in the interests of peace between Poland and Germany. Hitler promised a written reply the next day.

Meanwhile, appeals to keep the peace were made to Poland and Germany by the King of the Belgians, in the name of the Oslo Powers, by President Roosevelt, and by the Pope, in a broadcast from the Vatican. President Moscicki's answer gave emphatic assurance that Poland held the principles of peace voiced by these appeals.

The Polish Government was kept fully informed of the Anglo-German negotiation. Beck received from Kennard the draft of the British reply to Hitler's message, and found it satisfactory. He authorized the British Government to "inform the German Government that Poland is ready to enter at once into direct discussions with Germany." [76] Nevertheless, the danger of a German surprise attack could not be overlooked. Movements of German troops along the northern and western frontiers of Poland, and German occupation of the whole territory of Slovakia on August 28, made it imperative for Poland to take precautionary counter-measures. On August 29, the Undersecretary of State, Szembek, informed the British and French ambassadors of the Polish Government's decision to order general mobilization. Both Kennard and Noël protested vigorously that such a drastic step might hamper negotiations with Germany. They did not deny the necessity of mobilization, but argued that it should not be publicized. On their insistence the mobilization, which could not be effected without the posting of notices, was postponed twenty-four hours. In informing the ambassadors of this concession, Beck stressed that in the event of immediate German aggression, some ten Polish divisions would be missing from the battlefront, which might greatly jeopardize the Polish defense.[77]

Meanwhile, the Anglo-German negotiations were reaching a critical point. Henderson was again received by Hitler on August 29. The reply that he was handed was highly disappointing. Hitler's attitude had become more uncompromising, and his demands on Poland had stepped up. Although he agreed to British mediation and to direct negotiations with Poland, he now demanded that a Polish plenipotentiary arrive in Berlin the next day. When Henderson pointed out that this sounded like an ultimatum, both Hitler and Ribbentrop, who was present at the interview, strongly protested.

The German answer to the British message was rightly called a "mendacious document." [78] It contained a long list of alleged Polish offenses, including the Polish Government's rejection of German proposals for solving the questions in dispute, measures aiming at the economic destruction of Danzig, mobilization, and the mistreatment and killing of many members of the German minority, all of this in accordance with the abusive German propaganda about Poland.[79] It claimed boldly that "the German government never had any intention of touching Poland's vital interests," although the secret protocol signed on August 23 with Soviet Russia provided for practically another partition of Poland.

In conclusion, Hitler announced that a German draft proposal for resolving the dispute would be prepared and, if possible, handed to the British Government.

Clearly Hitler did not expect—nor did he wish—the arrival of a Polish plenipotentiary in Berlin within twenty-four hours. The demand was made to put the onus on Poland for not accepting negotiation and to prove to the German people that every effort had been made to avoid war. Hitler had firmly decided to attack Poland and only feared that some mediator would interfere with his plans. Compliance with the demands would not have altered the course of events.[80]

The British cabinet judged the demand for the arrival of a Polish plenipotentiary on August 30 as "wholly unreasonable," informed the German Government of this opinion, and in no way pressed the Polish Government to send a delegate, who would in all probability find himself in a situation similar to that faced by Schuschnigg, Hacha, and Urbsys. The answer that Henderson was instructed to communicate to Hitler insisted on normal procedure —that is, that the German proposals be handed to the Polish Ambassador for transmission to his government. Furthermore, the British Government made express reservations on demands put forward in the German reply, announced that the proposals would have to be "fully examined during the discussions," and gave the Germans to understand that the proposals would have to be compatible with the conditions stated by Great Britain and accepted in principle by Germany.[81]

Kennard was instructed to acquaint Beck with the British Government's attitude and to show him the draft of the British memorandum. Invited to express his views, Beck confirmed again the Polish Government's readiness to negotiate directly with Germany. He also gave assurance that during the negotiations Poland would not violate the German frontiers, provided that the Germans gave an identical guarantee of Polish territory. He suggested that a *modus vivendi,* negotiated with the help of Burckhardt, should be agreed upon in Danzig. Beck's only reservation concerned the international guarantee proposed by Great Britain, on which he wished to obtain more complete information. Finally, he assured Kennard that the Polish Government would do everything in its power to facilitate British efforts to save the peace.

It may be deduced from the documents published to date that at this stage of its mediatory action the British Government realized that the chances for peace were faint, indeed. It intensified its efforts to bring Poles and Germans together at the conference table, and strove to assure equal treatment for any Polish delegation.

The British reply to Hitler's statement of August 29 was communicated to Ribbentrop by Henderson on August 30 at midnight. Henderson suggested that the German proposals for a settlement should be handed to the Polish Ambassador for transmission to his government. Ribbentrop replied by rapidly reading aloud in German a long document of sixteen points, allegedly the "peace proposals" that Hitler intended to present to the Poles. When Henderson asked for the text, Ribbentrop refused, saying that it was too late as no Polish plenipotentiary had arrived before midnight. Ribbentrop also turned down brusquely Henderson's suggestion that he summon Lipski and hand him the proposal.[82]

The main points of this document were the immediate annexation of Danzig by Germany and a plebiscite to be held in the Corridor, whose boundaries were to be extended considerably southward. All persons domiciled in this territory on January 1, 1918, would be entitled to vote. Thus, the Poles established or born there after that date would be excluded from the plebiscite, while thousands of German colonists or members of the German administration and Army who after World War I had voluntarily returned to the Reich would be entitled to vote. These and other equally treacherous provisions show the perfidy of the German peace proposals, which at first glance seemed not unreasonable.[83]

Immediately after his conversation with Ribbentrop, Henderson gave Lipski an account of it and urged him to apply at once for an interview with the German Foreign Minister in order to avoid a breach. Similar suggestions were made to Beck by the British and French governments through their ambassadors in Warsaw. After consulting his government, Beck instructed Lipski to establish contact with Ribbentrop and to inform him that Poland looked favorably on the principle of direct negotiation. Lipski asked for an interview at 1 P.M., but was not received until 6:30. The meeting was brief. Ribbentrop inquired whether he was coming as a plenipotentiary with full powers, and Lipski replied that he came as Polish Ambassador to make a statement in the name of his government. Ribbentrop made no comment and said he would report the Ambassador's statement to Hitler. Ribbentrop's failure to hand Lipski the text of the German sixteen points, or show them to him, proved that they were meant as a stratagem to confuse world opinion and to put on Poland the onus of rejecting peace proposals—proposals that were never actually communicated to the Polish Government.

At 9 P.M., the sixteen points were broadcast by the German radio with a propaganda commentary. At 9:15, Weizsäcker finally handed a copy to Henderson and—within the next hour—to Coulondre and the American, Japanese, and Soviet representatives. This indicated that an attack on Poland was imminent.

Another German subterfuge was used to make it appear that Poland had provoked the war. A plan conceived earlier by the Gestapo was carried out with the help of the army during the night of August 31. A group of SS men and concentration-camp inmates, all wearing Polish uniforms, simulated a raid on the radio station of the Silesian frontier town of Gleiwitz. Several of the participating camp prisoners were shot and left dead in the building to make the attack look real. This was "the propagandist reason for war, no matter whether . . . plausible or not" that Hitler had promised the army commanders in his speech of August 23.[84]

At 4:45 in the morning of September 1, Hitler's "Directive No. 1 for the conduct of war" went into effect. Without a declaration of war, German armies crossed the Polish frontier in simultaneous attacks from the north, west, and south, and the Luftwaffe launched indiscriminate air raids on military objectives, open cities, villages, and roads.[85] "Never can there have been or ever be a case of more premeditated and carefully planned aggression."[86]

Acting on instructions from their government, the Polish ambassadors in Paris and London that same morning notified the French and British governments of the German aggression. They stated that this was a simple case of unprovoked attack and justified immediate application of the *casus foederis* provided by the Anglo-Polish and Franco-Polish treaties. Both allied governments took the same view. Henderson was instructed to warn the German Government that, unless German armies withdrew from Polish territory, Great Britain would fulfill her obligations to Poland.

A similar statement was made by France. The declaration of war, however, was delayed by a last-minute Italian initiative, favorably viewed by France, for calling an international conference aimed at general appeasement. Since no reply was forthcoming from the German Government and intense fighting continued along the whole front, Beck requested immediate fulfillment of their obligations by the allies. On September 3 at 9 A.M., the British Government presented Germany with a two-hour ultimatum. Not having received the demanded answer by 11 A.M., it declared a state of war with Germany. The French declaration of war followed a few hours later, going into effect at 5 P.M.

These moves by the Western powers were greeted with enthusiasm and relief by the Poles. Their morale, severely affected by the continuous bombing and the resulting disorganization, rose with the expectation of help from the West. The attitudes of Poland's neighbors were perplexing, however. Fears that Hungary would yield to German pressures were dispelled at the very start of the war. The Hungarian Government, faithful to the traditional Hungarian-Polish friendship, refused the right of passage to German troops attacking Poland. Rumania, Latvia, and Lithuania adopted strict neutrality.

The reaction of the Soviet Union to the German aggression did not at first indicate a change of attitude toward Poland. When the Polish Ambassador officially notified the Soviet Government of the German attack and the resulting state of war between Poland and Germany, Molotov did not question Grzybowski's statement on the unprovoked aggression, and thereby indirectly recognized its validity. He seemed to be skeptical about the possibility of French and British intervention. At the same time, the Soviet Ambassador to Poland, Sharonov, suggested negotiations on the purchase by

Poland of raw materials and munitions from the Soviet Union.[87] But when, on September 8, Grzybowski approached Molotov on this matter, he met with a refusal. He was told that, in the completely changed situation, Poland was, in the eyes of Moscow, synonymous with Great Britain and that the Soviet Union wished to remain outside the conflict.

Nine days later, on September 17, without declaring war, Soviet armies invaded Polish territory. At 2 A.M. on that day, Deputy-Commissar Potemkin presented a note to Grzybowski containing a unilateral abrogation of the Russian agreements with Poland.[88]

From that moment, the defeat of Poland was inevitable. Help from the Western allies could no longer be expected, and the Polish troops were unable to withstand the two powerful armies attacking them simultaneously from west and east. The Polish Government, which had been evacuated to the southeastern part of the country, found itself practically surrounded by rapidly advancing enemy detachments and decided to ask Rumania for asylum.[89]

The destruction of the Polish state and the partition of Poland's territory did not bring about the surrender of the nation. The Polish people continued the struggle, organizing an underground army and administration at home as well as a government and an army in exile abroad. Polish diplomacy had aligned Poland with France and Great Britain. This nucleus of three nations expanded in the course of World War II into a powerful coalition of many nations, whose final triumph over the aggressor was beyond doubt. That Poland should suffer a "defeat in victory" [90] was due to adverse circumstances over which neither the nation nor its diplomacy had control.

Notes

Chapter I: The Rebirth of the State

1. Dates of recognition: France, September 20, 1917; Great Britain, October 15, 1917; Italy, October 30, 1917; United States, November 10, 1917.

2. Address by the President of the United States delivered before a joint session of Congress on January 8, 1918. *Congressional Record 1918*, House Doc. 765, LVI, 681.

3. On the occasion of an inter-Allied conference held at Versailles on June 3, 1918, the prime ministers of France, Great Britain, and Italy agreed to that declaration. U.S. Department of State, *Papers Relating to the Foreign Relations of the United States, 1918* (Washington, D.C.: Government Printing Office), I, supp. 1, 810. (Hereafter cited as *Papers*.)

4. Besides his energetic and efficient diplomatic activity, consisting mainly of personal contacts with top European and American statesmen, Roman Dmowski, Chairman of the Polish National Committee, endeavored to acquaint Western public opinion with the problems of Central and Eastern Europe. His viewpoint on these questions was presented in a privately printed publication, *Problems of Central and Eastern Europe* (London, 1917).

5. An agreement between the French Government and the Polish National Committee signed in Paris on September 28, 1918, established the status of the Polish Army. Stanislas Filasiewicz, *La Question Polonaise* (Paris: Section d'Etudes et de Publications Politiques du Comité National Polonais, 1920), Doc. 257, p. 535.

6. Paul Roth, *Die Entstehung des Polnischen Staates* (Berlin: O. Liebmann, 1926), p. 129.

7. Of the 1,373 volunteers who enlisted until the annulment of the recruiting order, 697 were accepted, 296 were declared unfit for military service, and 380 did not appear at the Medical Commission.

8. Stanislaw Glabinski, a prominent member of the National Democratic party of Galicia, was appointed Minister of Foreign Affairs in the Swiezynski cabinet by the Regency Council on October 26, 1918.

9. U.S. Department of State, *Foreign Relations of the United States, 1919* (Washington, D.C.: Government Printing Office), II, 741. (Hereafter cited as *Foreign Relations*.)

10. The German Army in the Ukraine alone consisted of thirteen divisions and fifty-seven battalions. Max von Baden, *Erinnerungen und Dokumente* (Stuttgart: Deutsche Verlagsanstalt, 1927), II, 272.

11. Kessler had been one of the two officers to announce to Pilsudski in the Magdeburg prison on November 8, 1918, that he was free. He also took care of Pilsudski's and Sosnkowski's transportation to Poland. The real intention of the German Government in sending Kessler to Poland as a plenipotentiary seems to have been to hamper Poland's role as an Allied nation and to force a neutral status on her. Roth, *op. cit.*, pp. 32–33.

12. Casimir Smogorzewski, *L'Union Sacrée Polonaise* (Paris: A Costes, 1929), p. 30.

13. David H. Miller, *Diary of the Peace Conference* (New York: privately printed, 1924), XVI, 462.

14. Lithuania, Latvia, and Estonia, parts of Russia in 1914, had been occupied by German armies during the war and were destined to serve Germany's political aims in the Baltic region. After the defeat of the Central powers each of them strove to organize an independent national existence.

15. *Treaty of Versailles*, Art. 87, Par. 3.

16. Viscount d'Abernon, *The Eighteenth Decisive Battle of the World* (London: Hodder and Stoughton, 1931).

17. Hans Freiherr von Hammerstein, *Der Waffenstillstand 1918–1919 und Polen* (Berlin: Deutsche Verlagsgesellschaft für Politik und Geschichte, 1928).

18. Kazimierz Kumaniecki, *Odbudowa Panstwowosci Polskiej* (Kraków: J. Czernecki, 1924), p. 382.

19. For text of memorandum see Roth, *op. cit.*, pp. 133–51.

20. The commission was known as the Noulens Mission from the name of its Chairman, the French Ambassador to Russia. It remained in Poland until the end of March, 1919, and was dissolved soon afterward by the Supreme Council.

21. "Mr. Dmowski appeared before the Conference and in a long and exceedingly able speech, delivered first in pure and idiomatic French and afterwards repeated in perfect English, presented the case of Poland." David Lloyd George, *Memoirs of the Peace Conference* (New Haven, Conn.: Yale University Press, 1939), p. 631.

22. *Ibid.*, p. 637.

23. Henry Wickham Steed, *Through Thirty Years* (Garden City, N.Y.: Doubleday, Page and Co., 1924), II, 275.

24. Titus Komarnicki, *Rebirth of the Polish Republic* (London: William Heinemann Ltd., 1957), p. 320.

25. France, Comité d'Etudes, "Questions Européennes," *Travaux du Comité d'Etudes* (Paris: Imprimerie Nationale, 1919), II, 326.

26. John W. Wheeler Bennett, *The Forgotten Peace of Brest Litovsk* (New York: Macmillan and Co., 1938), Appendix X, p. 447.

27. Pologne, Ministère des Affaires Etrangères, *Documents Diplomatiques Concernant les Relations Polono-Lithuaniennes*, Décembre, 1918–Septembre, 1920 (Varsovie: Imprimerie de l'Etat, 1920), Doc. 4, p. 6.

28. Kumaniecki, *op. cit.*, Doc. 116, pp. 256–58.

29. General Ironside (W.E.I.) evaluates the increase of the Soviet troops facing the Poles from seven divisions in January, 1920, to twenty divisions and three cavalry divisions in March, 1920. *Encyclopaedia Britannica*, 14th ed., XIX, 765.

30. *Papers, 1920, op. cit.*, III, 371–75.

31. Komarnicki, *op. cit.*, p. 522.

32. *Papers, 1920, op. cit.*, III, 376–77.

33. H. W. V. Temperley (ed.), *A History of the Peace Conference in Paris* (London: H. Frowde and Hodder and Stoughton, 1920–24), VI, 319.

34. Stanislaw Grabski, *The Polish-Soviet Frontier* (London: privately printed, 1943), p. 23.

35. Pilsudski's manifesto to the inhabitants of the Ukraine was published on April 26, 1920. Kumaniecki, *op. cit.*, Doc. 121, pp. 266–67.

36. General Brussilov's appeal to the officers of the former Russian Army in *New York Times*, July 7, 1920, p. 17.

37. A Council of National Defense, Rada Obrony Panstwa, with Pilsudski as chairman was constituted; it was given power to decide questions pertaining to the conduct of war and the conclusion of peace. *Official Journal of the Polish Republic* (Dz. U.R.P.), No. 53 (July 1, 1920), p. 327.

38. In Great Britain the "Hands off Russia" action committee of the Labour Party exerted a strong influence on public opinion against Poland.

39. Carlo Sforza, *Diplomatic Europe Since the Treaty of Versailles* (New Haven, Conn.: Institute of Politics Publications, 1928), p. 21.

40. Jane Degras (ed.), *Soviet Documents on Foreign Policy* (Oxford: Oxford University Press, 1951), I, 194–97.

41. Political adversaries of Pilsudski endeavored to minimize his role in the elaboration of the strategic plan that led the Polish Army to victory. They attributed the authorship of the battle plan to Weygand. Weygand himself denied it. Casimir Smogorzewski, *La Pologne Restaurée* (Paris: Gebethner and Wolff, 1927), pp. 151–52.

42. *League of Nations Treaty Series* (hereafter cited as *LNTS*) 1921, Vol. VI, No. 149.

43. *LNTS, loc. cit.*, Art. 3.

Chapter II: The Shaping of Foreign Policy

1. According to the Constitution of 1921, Parliament was elected by universal suffrage and consisted of the Seym (Lower House) and the Senate (Upper House). The President of the Republic was elected for seven years by a joint session of both Houses, convened under the name of National Assembly for this purpose. The historical name of Seym (Diet) was currently applied to the Parliament as a whole.

2. The representatives of the American Relief Administration arrived in Warsaw on January 4, 1919. Within a few days they completed estimates on Poland's food requirements, and on February 17, the first American shiploads of flour were arriving in Danzig. A detailed account of the work of American agencies in Poland at that time is in H. H. Fisher, *America and the New Poland* (New York: The Macmillan Company, 1928), pp. 214–37.

3. Pilsudski's *coup d'état* took place on May 12, 1926. Three days later President Wojciechowski resigned to avoid further bloodshed. On May 31, the National Assembly elected Pilsudski President. He declined to accept the office. The next day Professor Ignacy Moscicki was elected and took the oath of office on June 4.

4. The political agreement between France and Poland was signed in Paris on February 19, 1921, and registered with the League of Nations Secretariat. *LNTS* 1923, Vol. XVIII, No. 449. The Franco-Polish military convention was kept secret by both governments. A probable text has been reconstructed from various sources by Piotr Wandycz in "Sojusz Polsko-Francuski z 1921," *Kultura* (Paris, 1959), No. 11/145, pp. 121–22.

5. Text of the Convention for a Defensive Alliance betwen the Polish Re-

public and the Kingdom of Rumania of March 3, 1921, in Arnold J. Toynbee, *Survey of International Affairs 1920–1923* (London: Oxford University Press, 1927), pp. 504–5; in the same volume (pp. 502–3) the agreement is published, by which the principal Allied and Associated Powers recognized Rumania's sovereign rights over Bessarabia.

6. *The Times* (London), August 5, 1920, cited by Wladyslaw Wielhorski in *Polska i Litwa* (London: The Polish Research Centre, 1947), p. 332.

7. Pilsudski admitted later that General Zeligowski had acted on his orders. Adam Zoltowski, *Border of Europe* (London: Hollis and Carter, 1950), p. 222.

8. Republic of Poland, Ministry of Foreign Affairs, *Official Documents Concerning Polish-German and Polish-Soviet Relations 1933–1939*, Polish White Book (London: Hutchinson and Co., n.d.), Doc. 149, pp. 165–68. (Hereafter cited as *Polish White Book.*)

9. Komarnicki, *op. cit.*, pp. 738–39.

10. Julian Lukasiewicz, *Z Doswiadczen Przeszlosci* (Biblioteka Orla Bialego, n.p., n.d.), pp. 5–6.

11. These activities reached their peak in the summer of 1924. A band of 160 men attacked the important railway station of Stolpce on the main Warsaw-Moscow line. Several weeks later, a similar raid took place on Luniniec, a town situated some 50 miles inland from the frontier.

12. *Supra*, p. 23.

13. Richard Breyer, *Das Deutsche Reich und Polen* (Würzburg: Holzner Verlag, 1955), p. 28, n. 38.

14. John B. Mason, *The Danzig Dilemma* (Stanford, Calif.: Stanford University Press, 1946), pp. 152–68.

15. During the Soviet-Polish war of 1920, Poland encountered the greatest difficulties in unloading shipments of ammunition in the port of Danzig.

16. Amadeo Giannini, *La Question de Danzig* (Roma: Instituto per l'Europa Orientale, 1933), p. 18.

17. Breyer, *op. cit.*, p. 28, n. 35.

18. F. P. Walters, *A History of the League of Nations* (London: Oxford University Press, 1952), I, 407.

19. *LNTS* 1922, Vol. XIX, No. 271.

20. *Frankfurter Zeitung*, June 14, 1925, as cited by Smogorzewski, *La Pologne Restaurée, op. cit.*, pp. 108–9.

21. United States National Archives, Department of State files No. 860c. 00/175. *Report* of the American Minister in Warsaw of February 15, 1923.

22. "Nothing, indeed, was more noticeable throughout the Council's proceedings in these years than the reasonable and conciliatory attitude of Poland. Polish affairs were constantly on the agenda." Walters, *op. cit.*, I, 304.

23. *Supra*, p. 34.

24. Envoy Extraordinary and Minister Plenipotentiary to Rumania 1919–22; Minister of Foreign Affairs, December, 1922 to May, 1923, and again July 27, 1924, to May 5, 1926; Prime Minister, November 20, 1925, to May 5, 1926.

25. Count Aleksander Skrzynski, *Poland and Peace* (London: G. Allen and Unwin, 1923), *passim*.

26. He made 19 speeches in 21 days. *Europe Nouvelle* (Paris, 1925), p. 1117.

27. Jan Chomecki [pseud.], "Briand-Stresemann-Skrzynski," *Przeglad Wspolczesny*, No. 122 (June, 1932), p. 410.

28. A. Bregman, *La Politique de la Pologne dans la Société des Nations* (Paris: F. Alcan, 1932), p. 15.

29. *Le Temps* (Paris), February 28, 1926, as cited in A. J. Toynbee, *Survey of International Affairs 1926* (London: Oxford University Press, 1928), p. 26.

Chapter III: The Quest for Stability

1. Colonel Józef Beck, *Dernier Rapport, Politique Polonaise 1926–1939* (Neuchâtel: Editions de la Baconnière, 1951), p. 3.

2. *Supra*, p. 37, n. 3.

3. He became Minister of Military Affairs, Inspector General of the Army, Commander in Chief of the Armed Forces in time of war.

4. *Le Matin* (Paris), May 26, 1926, as cited in Beck, *op. cit.*, pp. 3–4, n. 2.

5. Jules Laroche, *La Pologne de Pilsudski: Souvenirs d'une Ambassade 1926–1935* (Paris: Flammarion, 1953), p. 50.

6. *Ibid.*, pp. 48–49.

7. The rank of Marshal of Poland was bestowed on him on this occasion.

8. *Supra*, p. 39, n. 4.

9. Minister of Foreign Affairs Skrzynski and Minister of Military Affairs Sikorski had talks in Paris with French political and military leaders.

10. Georges Castellan, *Le Réarmement Clandestin du Reich 1930–1935* (Paris: Librarie Plon, 1954), p. 471.

11. In a letter to the Kronprinz, dated September 7, 1925, Stresemann listed among his objectives in seeking Germany's admission to the League of Nations the revision of the eastern frontier and the protection of German minorities. Breyer, *op. cit.*, p. 60.

12. Under Article 4, Paragraph 5 of the Covenant, a nation that was party to a problem was invited to take part in the Council's deliberations on it.

13. Beck, *op. cit.*, p. 19.

14. Walters, *op. cit.*, p. 399.

15. *Ibid.*, p. 385.

16. Laroche, *op. cit.*, p. 67.

17. "Striking the Council table with his clenched fist . . ." Walters, *op. cit.*, I, 408.

18. *Ibid.*, p. 409.

19. Mason, *op. cit.*, p. 215.

20. Karol Poznanski, "Wypadki Majowe Widziane od Strony Moskwy," *Wiadomosci* (London, 1957), XII, No. 586, 1.

21. Former Minister of Foreign Affairs (in 1920), Envoy Extraordinary and Minister Plenipotentiary to the U.S.S.R. from December, 1926, to December, 1932.

22. C. M. Gathorne-Hardy, *A Short History of International Affairs 1920–1939* (London: Oxford University Press, 1950), p. 349.

23. Wladyslaw Pobog-Malinowski, *Najnowsza Historia Polityczna Polski 1864–1945* (London: by the author, 1956), II, Part I, 534.

24. Robert Machray, *The Poland of Pilsudski* (London: G. Allen and Unwin, 1936), pp. 280–81.

25. Pobog-Malinowski, *op. cit.*, p. 540.

26. He succeeded Alfred Wysocki, who had been appointed Envoy Extraordinary and Minister Plenipotentiary to Germany.

Chapter IV: Efforts to Reinforce Security

1. Text of the agreement appears in J. W. Wheeler-Bennett (ed.), *Documents on International Affairs 1929* (London: Oxford University Press, 1933), pp. 153–55. Some Polish writers maintain that the liquidation agreement had been detrimental to Poland, e.g., Zygmunt Wojciechowski (ed.), *Poland's Place in Europe* (Poznan: Instytut Zachodni, 1947).

2. Józef Lipski, "Stosunki Polsko-Niemieckie przed Wybuchem Wojny w Swietle Aktow Norymberskich," *Sprawy Miedzynarodowe* (London: 1947), Nos. 2–3, p. 13.

3. "Paris Peace Conference 1919," *Foreign Relations*, XII, 119.

4. Machray, *op. cit.*, pp. 318–19.

5. Gathorne-Hardy, *op. cit.*, p. 367.

6. Ambassador Extraordinary and Plenipotentiary to Turkey 1933–36, to the United States 1936–40.

7. Beck, *op. cit.*, p. 41.

8. The German Foreign Office, designated by the name of its location.

9. Instructions given Wysocki for his communication to Hitler in Józef Lipski, "Przyczynki do Polsko-Niemieckiej Deklaracji o Nieagresji," *Bellona* (London, 1951), No. III, pp. 10–11.

10. *Polish White Book, op. cit.*, Doc. 6, pp. 16–19.

11. *Ibid.*, Doc. 7, p. 19.

12. Laroche, *op. cit.*, p. 135.

13. *Ibid.*, p. 141.

14. Józef Lipski, memorandum on instructions given by Pilsudski to Beck in Lipski's presence on November 20, 1933. (In the author's files.)

15. Marshal Tukhachevsky accepted an invitation from the German Army to attend maneuvers in September, 1932, but the Polish Military Attaché was not invited.

16. Boguslaw Miedzinski, "Polska Polityka Zagraniczna w Okresie Przedwojennym," *Wiadomosci* (London), October 26, 1952, No. 43/343, p. 1.

17. In March, 1934, the Soviet Government made an identical proposal to Hitler, who rejected it.

18. On Poland's demand, reference to the Locarno arbitration agreement was also omitted.

19. *Polish White Book, op. cit.*, Doc. 10, pp. 20–21.

20. Laroche, *op. cit.*, p. 147.

21. During the week following the signing of the Polish-German declaration, other foreign representatives called on Beck and Szembek. In his talk with the American Ambassador, Beck said: "Those among your countrymen who were worried about the Polish Corridor don't need to lose their sleep any more." (In the author's files.)

22. "I have just returned from the Quai d'Orsay. Massigli read to me Laroche's telegram on his conversation with Marshal Pilsudski. . . . The conclusion to be drawn from the talk I had with Massigli is that the conversation

of the Marshal with Laroche has helped clear the atmosphere and will have a decisive influence on the further development of the political situation." Semi-official letter of February 2, 1934, from Anatol Muhlstein, Minister-Counselor of the Polish Embassy in Paris, to the author. (In the author's files.)

23. Beck, *op. cit.*, p. 55.

24. Janusz Jedrzejewicz.

25. Hans Roos, *Polen und Europa* (Tübingen: J. C. B. Mohr, 1957), p. 114.

26. "Greiser looked, and was, an unmitigated villain. To Forster or anyone else who could help or harm him, he was slavishly obsequious: to many Danzigers, and later the millions of Poles whom fate put in his power, he was a monster of cruelty." Walters, *op. cit.*, II, 618.

27. *Polish White Book, op. cit.*, Doc. 157, pp. 179–80.

28. Léon Noël, *L'Aggression Allemande contre la Pologne* (Paris: Flammarion, 1946), p. 76.

29. Comte Jean Szembek, *Journal 1933–39* (Paris: Librairie Plon, 1952), pp. 3–7.

30. Laroche, *op. cit.*, pp. 155–62.

31. U.S. Department of State, *Documents on German Foreign Policy* (Washington, D.C.: Government Printing Office, 1958), Series C, I, January to October, 1933, Doc. 2, p. 3, and Doc. 34, p. 73. (Hereafter cited as *DGFP*.)

32. Noël, *op. cit.*, pp. 253–54.

33. Beck, *op. cit.*, pp. 281–83.

34. *Ibid.*, Doc. 8, pp. 335–38.

35. On March 16, 1935.

36. The declaration was made on September 13, 1934, five days before the admission of the U.S.S.R. to the League of Nations. Józef Beck, *Przemowienia, Deklaracje, Wywiady 1931–1939* (Warsaw: Gebethner i Wolff, 1939), pp. 128–31.

37. *Polish White Book, op. cit.*, Doc. 158, pp. 180–81.

38. Laroche, *op. cit.*, p. 59.

39. Roos, *op. cit.*, p. 205.

40. Beck, *Dernier Rapport*, p. 78.

41. *Ibid.*, p. 337, Paragraph 2 is directed implicitly at Lithuania, the only nation in East Europe without diplomatic relations with Poland.

42. Laroche, *op. cit.*, p. 160.

43. Beck, *op. cit.*, p. 337. Paragraph 3 of the memorandum on Poland's attitude toward the Eastern Pact plan, communicated to the French Government on September 27, 1934.

44. Hitler himself endeavored to strengthen this impression. *Polish White Book, op. cit.*, Doc. 13, 14, pp. 23–25.

45. Beck had already met Goebbels in Geneva. Beck, *op. cit.*, p. 30.

46. The Roehm affair took place on June 30, 1933, Dollfuss' assassination on July 25, 1933.

47. Roos, *op. cit.*, p. 150.

48. *Ibid.*, p. 181.

49. *Polish White Book, op. cit.*, Doc. 16, p. 26.

50. Szembek, *op. cit.*, p. 49.

51. Laroche, *op. cit.*, p. 206.

52. Pobog-Malinowski, *op. cit.*, p. 559, n. 40.

53. Stefan Benedykt, "Wspomnienia o Ostatnich Dniach Marszalka Pilsudskiego," *Wiadomosci* (London), June 19, 1955, No. 25/481.
54. Szembek, *op. cit.*, p. 55.
55. Record of conversation held on April 2 and 3, 1935, between Beck and Eden in Warsaw. (In the author's files.)
56. *Ibid.*
57. Walters, *op. cit.*, p. 612.
58. Szembek, *op. cit.*, p. 64.
59. Polish Commission for International Law Cooperation, *Constitution of the Republic of Poland* [April 23, 1935] (Warsaw, 1935).
60. In his dispatch No. 1660 of March 28, 1928, the American Minister to Poland reported on a conversation with Polakiewicz, a prominent member of the government party, whom Pilsudski had informed of his desire "to bring about a revision of the constitution along the lines of that of the United States, thereby increasing the power and strength of the Executive." In the *National Archives*, Washington, D.C., Box 9329, file 860c/00/430.

Chapter V: The Policy of Equilibrium

1. Pilsudski's confidence in and high opinion of Beck have been confirmed by many testimonies; Laroche, *op. cit.*, pp. 102–4; also a letter from former Prime Minister Jedrzejewicz quoted in Beck, *op. cit.*, p. 62.
2. Noël, *op. cit.*, p. 123.
3. Szembek, *op. cit.*, p. 89.
4. *Ibid.*, p. 106.
5. Beck, *op. cit.*, pp. 102–3; Szembek, *op. cit.*, pp. 109–11.
6. Machray, *op. cit.*, pp. 419–20.
7. In 1926, 36 votes; 1932, 41 votes; 1935, 47 votes.
8. W. A. Zbyszewski, "Fragmenty Pamietnikow Min. Szembeka," *Kultura* (Paris, 1952), No. 6/56, p. 50.
9. Noël, *op. cit.*, p. 125; Beck, *op. cit.*, p. 113.
10. Beck, *op. cit.*, p. 114, n. 2.
11. Józef Lipski, "Stosunki Polsko-Niemieckie . . . ," *op. cit.*, p. 16.
12. Hitler's Reichstag speech, March 7, 1936.
13. *LNTS* 1926, LIV, No. 1292, 291–97, Art. 4.
14. Walters, *op. cit.*, II, 698.
15. *Supra*, p. 94.
16. Georges Bonnet, *Défense de la Paix*, II, *Fin d'une Europe* (Geneva: Edition du Cheval Blanc, 1948), pp. 135–36.
17. Jan Starzewski, "Studium Polski Wspolczesnej: Polska Polityka Zagraniczna w Latach 1914–1939," Szkola Nauk Politycznych i Spolecznych (London: mimeographed manuscript, 1950).
18. Roos, *op. cit.*, p. 55.
19. The Polish Minister in Bucharest, Miroslaw Arciszewski, contributed to the fall of Titulescu. Warsaw, however, did not approve of this action. Szembek, *op. cit.*, p. 119.
20. Roos, *op. cit.*, pp. 269–70.
21. Beck, *op. cit.*, p. 119.
22. *Supra*, p. 102.

23. The accord was often called the "Rambouillet Agreement" because it was signed during a reception given by the President of the French Republic in honor of Smigly-Rydz at the Rambouillet Palace.

24. Polskie Sily Zbrojne, *Kampania Wrzesniowa 1939* (London: Instytut Historyczny im. Gen. Sikorskiego, 1951), I, 92. Général Gamelin, *Servir, Le Prologue du Drame* (Paris: Librarie Plon, 1946), p. 228.

25. Noël, *op. cit.*, p. 144; Gamelin, *op. cit.*, pp. 232–33.

26. Szembek, *op. cit.*, pp. 191–201.

27. Walters, *op. cit.*, p. 621.

28. Józef Lipski, "Nowe Przyczynki dotyczace Wybuchu Wojny Polsko-Niemieckiej w 1939 r," *Bellona* (London, 1950), I, pp. 18 ff.

29. From February 18, 1937, to the outbreak of World War II.

30. *Polish White Book, op. cit.*, Doc. 38, p. 45.

31. Lipski, "Nowe Przyczynki . . . ," *op. cit.*, pp. 21–22.

32. *Supra*, p. 51.

33. *Supra*, p. 85.

34. *Polish White Book, op. cit.*, Doc. 32, p. 40.

35. Szembek, *op. cit.*, p. 248; Beck, *op. cit.*, p. 145.

36. Count Szembek's letter to the author of April 12, 1938. (In the author's files.)

37. Beck, *op. cit.*, p. 147.

38. Noël, *op. cit.*, p. 184.

39. Roos, *op. cit.*, p. 276.

40. March 11, 1938.

41. R. G. D. Laffan and others, *Survey of International Affairs 1938* (London: Oxford University Press, 1953), III, 347–53.

42. Monica Curtis (ed.), *Documents on International Affairs 1938* (London: Oxford University Press, 1942), I, 302–3.

43. *DGFP*, Series D, V, Doc. 329, pp. 433–34.

44. R. G. D. Laffan and others, *op. cit.*, p. 46.

45. Boris Celovsky, *Das Münchener Abkommen 1938* (Stuttgart: Deutsche Verlags-Anstalt, 1958), p. 104.

46. Beck, *op. cit.*, p. 148; Szembek, *op. cit.*, p. 299.

47. *DGFP*, Series D, II, Doc. 319, pp. 518–19.

48. Georges Bonnet, *Défense de la Paix.* Vol. I. *De Washington au Quai d'Orsay* (Geneva: Bibliothèque du Cheval Ailé, Constant Bourquin, ed., 1948), pp. 237 and 242.

49. Stefan Osusky, "Events Leading to Munich," Letter to the Editor, *New York Times*, October 20, 1958, p. 28.

50. *Supra*, p. 17.

51. Noël, *op. cit.*, p. 206.

52. Great Britain, *Documents on British Foreign Policy 1919–1939*, Third Series, III, Encl. 1, Doc. 20, p. 14. (Hereafter cited as *DBFP*.)

53. *Ibid.*, Encl. 2; also Juliusz Lukasiewicz, "Sprawa Czechoslowacka w 1938 r.na tle Stosunkow Polsko-Francuskich," *Sprawy Miedzynarodowe* (London, 1948), Rok II, Nos. 2–3/ 6–7, p. 49.

54. *DBFP*, Third Series, III, Doc. 21, pp. 15–16.

55. Beck, *op. cit.*, Docs. 11, 12, pp. 342–44.

56. *DBFP*, Third Series, III, Doc. 55, p. 40.

57. *Ibid.*, annexes to Doc. 101, pp. 69–73.
58. *Ibid.*, Doc. 136, p. 104.
59. John W. Wheeler-Bennett, *Munich: Prologue to Tragedy* (New York: Duell, Sloan & Pearce, 1948), map facing p. 461.
60. *DGFP*, V, Doc. 61, pp. 83–84.
61. Walters, *op. cit.*, p. 782.
62. Degras, *op. cit.*, III, 305.
63. *Polish White Book, op. cit.*, Doc. 160, pp. 181–82.

Chapter VI: Toward the World Conflict

1. *Trial of the Major War Criminals before the International Military Tribunal, Nuremberg 1945–1946.* Proceedings and Documents in evidence, 42 Vols. (Nuremberg International Military Tribunal, 1947–49), Vol. XXV, Doc. 386 PS, pp. 402–13.
2. *Polish White Book, op. cit.*, Doc. 44, pp. 47–48; *DGFP*, V, Doc. 86, pp. 113–14.
3. Hitler's Reichstag Speech, February 20, 1938, extracts in *Polish White Book, op. cit.*, Doc. 37, p. 44; also Doc. 147, p. 142.
4. *Trials of War Criminals before the Nürnberg Military Tribunals*, Vol. XIII, "The Ministries Case," U.S. v. von Weizsäcker (Nürnberg Military Tribunals, October 1946–April 1949), Doc. NG–5870, p. 3.
5. *Supra*, p. 91.
6. Polish Institute of International Affairs, "Misja hr. Czakyego w Warszawie, 5–6 Pazdziernika 1938 r." *Sprawy Miedzynarodowe* (Warsaw, 1958), XI, Nos. 7–8, July–August, pp. 71–73.
7. *Supra*, p. 122.
8. *Polish White Book, op. cit.*, Doc. 46, pp. 50–52; *DGFP*, V, Doc. 101, pp. 127–29.
9. *Polish White Book, op. cit.*, Doc. 48, pp. 53–54.
10. Noël, *op. cit.*, pp. 253–54.
11. *DBFP*, IV, Doc. 175, p. 181.
12. *The von Hassel Diaries* (Garden City, N.Y.: Doubleday, 1947), p. 53.
13. *Supra*, 112.
14. In the fall of 1938, German authorities deported to the Polish border and concentrated in the "no man's land" area several thousand Jews, many of whom had spent all their lives in Germany. The pretext invoked by Germany was a Polish decree regulating the revalidation of passports of Polish citizens who had lived abroad for a long time. Although this is normal procedure, followed by most countries, the measure was ill-timed; it supplied the German Government, at a time of anti-Semitic excesses in Germany, with a pretext for deporting Jews they considered Polish citizens. The Polish authorities, faced with a large-scale, unexpected immigration, endeavored, in cooperation with Jewish organizations, to organize help for the unfortunate deportees and to cope with all the problems involved (contacting their families, etc.). They admitted some 15,000 persons to Poland. They also took retaliatory measures against German citizens in Poland, whereupon the deportations from Germany were suspended. In later Polish-German negotiations, the

expelled Jews obtained the right to re-enter Germany to arrange or liquidate their personal and business problems.

15. *DBFP*, IV, Doc. 178, pp. 182–83.

16. R. G. D. Laffan and others, *op. cit.*, Part 1.

17. Winston S. Churchill, *The Second World War: The Gathering Storm* (Boston, Mass.: Houghton Mifflin Company, 1948), p. 345.

18. *Polish White Book, op. cit.*, Doc. 61, p. 63.

19. *DBFP*, IV, Doc. 446, p. 400.

20. *Ibid.*, Doc. 518, p. 500; *Polish White Book, op. cit.*, Doc. 66, pp. 70–71.

21. *DBFP*, IV, Doc. 566, p. 545 and Doc. 571, p. 547.

22. *Polish White Book, op. cit.*, Doc. 69, p. 72.

23. *DBFP*, IV, Doc. 458, p. 422.

24. *Polish White Book, op. cit.*, Doc. 147, p. 144.

25. *Ibid.*, Doc. 62, p. 64 and Doc. 63, p. 69.

26. *Ibid.*, Doc. 64, p. 69.

27. *DGFP*, VI, Doc. 99, p. 117.

28. Beck, *op. cit.*, pp. 190–91, n. 2.

29. Szembek, *op. cit.*, p. 434.

30. *DBFP*, V, Doc. 16, pp. 47–49.

31. *Polish White Book, op. cit.*, Doc. 70, p. 73.

32. *DGFP*, VI, Doc. 149, p. 186. Arnold Toynbee (ed.), *Documents on International Affairs 1939–1946* (London: Oxford University Press, 1951), I, 130–34. (Hereafter cited as *Documents 1939–1946*.)

33. France, Ministère des Affaires Etrangères, *Le Livre Jaune Français* (Paris: Imprimerie Nationale, 1939), Doc. 92, p. 125.

34. Including the U.S.S.R., the Baltic states, and the Balkan Entente.

35. He feared this would interfere with the plan to include the U.S.S.R. in the "peace front."

36. *DGFP*, VI, Doc. 173, p. 210.

37. *Documents 1939–1946*, I, 204–7.

38. *Ibid.*, pp. 214–56.

39. *DBFP*, V, Doc. 313, p. 370.

40. *Polish White Book, op. cit.*, Doc. 77, pp. 84–88 and Doc. 78, pp. 88–92. An analysis of Beck's speech is in *DBFP*, V, Doc. 386, pp. 440–42. For German proposals to join in an expedition against the U.S.S.R. see J. Lipski, "Nowe Przyczynki Dotyczace Wybuchu Wojny Polsko-Niemieckiej w 1939 r.," *Bellona* (London, 1950), I, 27.

41. On May 30, 1939, Beck asked Szembek if he would accept the post of Ambassador to Germany. Szembek said he would. He considered it a duty and an honor to serve his country's interests under the most difficult circumstances. Szembek, *op. cit.*, pp. 465–66. Also a letter of June 13, 1939, addressed to the author. (In the author's files.)

42. Kennard evaluated the pertinent monthly expenses at more than £2 million. *DBFP*, V, Doc. 266, p. 283.

43. *Ibid.*, Doc. 508, pp. 540–41, enclosure.

44. Polish viewpoint on the inacceptability of the conditions in *DBFP*, VI, Doc. 340, p. 378.

45. *DGFP*, VII, Doc. 192, p. 293. *Trial of the Major War Criminals, op. cit.*, XIV, Doc. 798–PS, pp. 64–65.

46. Polskie Sily Zbrojne, *op. cit.*, p. 94.
47. Général Gamelin, *op. cit.*, II, 414.
48. *Ibid.*, pp. 417–18. L. B. Namier, *Diplomatic Prelude* (London: Macmillan & Co. Ltd., 1948), pp. 465–66.
49. It was signed only on September 4, 1939. *Polish White Book, op. cit.*, Doc. 139, pp. 137–38.
50. *DBFP*, VI, Doc. 374, pp. 415–19.
51. U.S. Department of State, *Nazi-Soviet Relations 1939–1941*, ed. by Raymond James Sontag and James Stuart Beddie (Washington, D.C.: Government Printing Office, 1948), p. 1.
52. France, *Le Livre Jaune, op. cit.*, Doc. 123, pp. 155–57.
53. Starzewski, *op. cit.*, p. 74.
54. *Foreign Relations 1939*, I, 331–32.
55. *Polish White Book, op. cit.*, Doc. 163, p. 183.
56. Starzewski, *op. cit.*, pp. 73–74.
57. *DBFP*, V, Doc. 601, p. 658.
58. *Ibid.*, VI, Annex 1, pp. 780–82, par. 17.
59. Both those "gates" were the historic avenues of Russian invasions. *Supra*, p. 25.
60. *DBFP*, VII, Doc. 176, p. 150.
61. *Ibid.*, Doc. 251, p. 203.
62. France, *Le Livre Jaune*, Doc. 150, pp. 205–6; Great Britain, *Documents Concerning German-Polish Relations and the Outbreak of Hostilities Between Great Britain and Germany on September 3, 1939* (London: H.M.S.O., 1939), Doc. 35, p. 76. (Hereafter cited as *Cmd. 6106.*)
63. *DGFP*, VI, Doc. 774, p. 1070.
64. Namier, *op. cit.*, p. 420.
65. *DBFP*, VI, Doc. 659, Annex, p. 695.
66. Great Britain, Foreign Office, *Agreement Between the Government of the United Kingdom and the Polish Government Regarding Mutual Assistance* (with Protocol), (London: H.M.S.O., 1945), Cmd. 6616, Art. 5, p. 3.
67. *Ibid.*, p. 4.
68. The conversation with Henderson is reported in *DBFP*, VII, Docs. 283, 284, pp. 227–31; with Coulondre in France, *Le Livre Jaune*, Doc. 242, pp. 312–14.
69. Namier, *op. cit.*, p. 330.
70. *DGFP*, VII, Doc. 119, pp. 129–30, and n. 1; there is documentary evidence of various provocations, *ibid.*, Doc. 128, p. 137.
71. *Ibid.*, Doc. 197, p. 208.
72. France, *Le Livre Jaune*, Doc. 269.
73. *Polish White Book, op. cit.*, Doc. 147, pp. 147–48.
74. A. Toynbee and V. M. Toynbee (eds.), *Survey of International Affairs, The Eve of War 1939* (London: Oxford University Press, 1958), p. 544. Lord Halifax, *Fullness of Days* (New York: Dodd, Mead, 1957), p. 213.
75. *DBFP*, VII, Doc. 426, pp. 330–32.
76. *Ibid.*, Doc. 420, p. 328.
77. Beck, *op. cit.*, p. 218. *DBFP*, VII, Doc. 492, pp. 375–76.
78. Namier, *op. cit.*, p. 354. *DBFP*, VII, Doc. 502, pp. 388–90.
79. *Ibid.*, Doc. 367, pp. 297–98. The Polish Government protested against

the German campaign of slander in an official communiqué: *Polish White Book, op. cit.*, Doc. 94, p. 106.

80. *DGFP*, VII, Doc. 192, p. 204.

81. *DBFP*, VII, Doc. 543, pp. 413–14.

82. *Ibid.*, Doc. 574, pp. 432–33. Text in *Ibid.*, Doc. 622, pp. 459–62. Analysis from the viewpoint of Polish diplomacy in Lipski, *Sprawy Miedzynarodowe, op. cit.*, No. 4, pp. 48–49.

83. Text of Beck's instructions to Polish representatives abroad in *Polish White Book, op. cit.*, Doc. 110, p. 119.

84. *DGFP*, VII, Doc. 193, p. 205.

85. Noël, *op. cit.*, p. 481.

86. Sir Nevile Henderson, *Failure of a Mission: Berlin 1937–1939* (New York: G. P. Putnam's Sons, 1940), p. 293.

87. *Polish White Book, op. cit.*, Doc. 171, p. 187.

88. *Ibid.*, Doc. 175, pp. 189–90.

89. Beck, *op. cit.*, p. 241. In his memoirs, Beck refers to the arrangements he made with the Rumanian Ambassador to Poland regarding the right of passage of the President and Government of Poland through Rumanian territory. He declared on this occasion that, under the circumstances, no demand would be made on Rumania for the application of the stipulations of the Polish-Rumanian alliance providing for aid against Soviet aggression. In spite of the Rumanian offer of hospitality and promise of transit facilities, the Polish dignitaries were virtually interned.

90. Title of the book by Jan Ciechanowski, *Defeat in Victory* (Garden City, N.Y.: Doubleday, 1947), which aptly epitomizes the fate of Poland in World War II.

Selected Bibliography

OFFICIAL DOCUMENTS

CURTIS, MONICA (ed.). *Documents on International Affairs, 1938*. Royal Institute of International Affairs. London: Oxford University Press, 1942.

DEGRAS, JANE (ed.). *Soviet Documents on Foreign Policy*. Vol. III. London: Oxford University Press, 1951.

Documents and Materials Relating to the Eve of the Second World War. Vol. I (November, 1937–38). New York: International Publishers, 1948.

FRANCE, COMITÉ D'ETUDES. "Questions Européennes," *Travaux du Comité d'Etudes*. Vol. II. Paris: Imprimerie Nationale, 1919.

FRANCE, MINISTÈRE DES AFFAIRES ETRANGÈRES. *Le Livre Jaune Français, Documents Diplomatiques, 1938–1939*. Paris: Imprimerie Nationale, 1939.

GERMANY. *Documents on the Events Preceding the Outbreak of the War*. Berlin, 1939, New York, 1940: German Foreign Office.

———. *German White Book: Documents Concerning the Last Phase of the German-Polish Crisis*. New York: German Library of Information, 1939.

GREAT BRITAIN. *Documents Concerning German-Polish Relations and the Outbreak of Hostilities between Great Britain and Germany on September 3, 1939*. Cmd. 6106. London: His Majesty's Stationery Office, 1939.

POLAND, MINISTRY FOR FOREIGN AFFAIRS. *Official Documents concerning Polish-German and Polish-Soviet Relations, 1933–1939. The Polish White Book*. London: published by authority of the Polish Government by Hutchinson and Co., n.d.

RÉPUBLIQUE POLONAISE, MINISTÈRE DES AFFAIRES ETRANGÈRES. *Documents Diplomatiques concernant les Relations Polono-Lithuaniennes. (Décembre 1918–Septembre 1920)*. Varsovie: Imprimerie de l'Etat, 1920.

TOYNBEE, ARNOLD J. (ed.). *Documents on International Affairs, 1939–1946*. Vol. I. Royal Institute of International Affairs. London: Oxford University Press, 1951.

Trial of the Major War Criminals before the International Military Tribunal, Nuremberg, 1945–1946. Proceedings and documents in evidence. 42 vols. Nuremberg Military Tribunal, 1947–49.

Trials of War Criminals before the Nürnberg Military Tribunals, under Control Council Law No. 10. 15 vols. Nürnberg, October 1946–April 1949.

U.S. DEPARTMENT OF STATE. *Documents on German Foreign Policy, 1918–1945*. Series C, Vol. I; Series D, Vols. II, IV, V, VI, VII. Washington, D.C.: Government Printing Office, 1949–56.

U.S. DEPARTMENT OF STATE. *Foreign Relations of the United States. Diplo-*

matic Papers, 1931. Washington, D.C.: Government Printing Office, 1948.

U.S. DEPARTMENT OF STATE. *Papers Relating to the Foreign Relations of the United States, 1920–1931.* Washington, D.C.: Government Printing Office, 1935–46.

U.S. DEPARTMENT OF STATE. *Nazi-Soviet Relations, 1939–1941. Documents from the Archives of the German Foreign Office,* eds. Raymond James Sontag and James Stuart Beddie. Washington, D.C.: Government Printing Office, 1948.

WHEELER-BENNETT, JOHN W. (ed.). *Documents on International Affairs, 1930.* Royal Institute of International Affairs. London: Oxford University Press, 1931.

WOODWARD, E. L., and BUTLER, ROHAN (eds.). *Documents on British Foreign Policy, Third Series.* Vols. III, IV, V, VI, and VII. London: H.M.S.O., 1950–54.

BOOKS, MEMOIRS, AND OTHER WORKS

D'ABERNON, VISCOUNT. *The Eighteenth Decisive Battle of the World.* London: Hodder and Stoughton, 1931.

ASKENAZY, SIMON. *Danzig et la Pologne.* Paris: Librairie Felix Alcan, 1919.

AUGUR [VLADIMIR POLIAKOFF]. *Eagles Black and White.* London: Appleton and Co., 1929.

BADEN, MAX VON. *Erinnerungen und Dokumente.* Stuttgart: Deutsche Verlag-Anstalt, 1927.

BECK, COLONEL JOSEPH. *Dernier Rapport: Politique Polonaise: 1926–1939.* Neuchâtel: Editions de la Baconnière, 1951.

BECK, JÓZEF. *Przemowienia, Deklaracje, Wywiady: 1931–1939.* Warsaw: Gebethner i Wolff, 1939.

BONNET, GEORGES. *Défense de la Paix.* Vol. I: *De Washington au Quai d'Orsay,* ed. Constant Bourquin. Genève: Bibliothèque du Cheval Ailé, 1946; Vol. II: *Fin d'une Europe.* Genève: Editions du Cheval Blanc, 1948.

BREGMAN, A. *La Politique de la Pologne dans la Société des Nations.* Paris: F. Alcan, 1932.

BREYER, RICHARD. *Das Deutsche Reich und Polen: 1932–1937.* Aussenpolitik und Volksgruppenfragen. Würzburg: Holzner Verlag, 1955.

BUELL, RAYMOND L. *Poland: Key to Europe.* New York: Alfred A. Knopf, 1939.

BURIAN VON RAJECZ, STEPHEN. *Drei Jahre aus der Zeit meiner Amtsführung im Kriege.* Berlin: Ullstein, 1923.

CARDWELL, ANN SU. *Poland and Russia, The Last Quarter Century.* New York: Sheed and Ward, 1944.

CASTELLAN, GEORGES. *Le Réarmement Clandestin du Reich, 1930–1935.* Paris: Librarie Plon, 1954.

CELOVSKY, BORIS. *Das Münchener Abkommen von 1938.* Stuttgart: Deutsche Verlags-Anstalt, 1958.

CHURCHILL, WINSTON S. *The Second World War: The Gathering Storm.* Boston: Houghton Mifflin Company, 1948.

Ciano's Hidden Diary: 1937–1938. New York: E. P. Dutton and Co., 1953.

COULONDRE, ROBERT. *De Staline à Hitler: Souvenirs de Deux Ambassades, 1936–1939.* Paris: Hachette, 1950.

CRAIG, GORDON A., and GILBERT, FELIX (eds.). *The Diplomats: 1919–1939.* Princeton, N.J.: Princeton University Press, 1953.

DABSKI, JAN. *Pokoj Ryski. Wspomnienia. Pertraktacje. Tajne Uklady z Joffem. Listy.* Warsaw: privately printed, 1931.

DMOWSKI, ROMAN. *La Question Polonaise.* Paris: A. Colin, 1909.

———. *Problems of Central and Eastern Europe.* London: privately printed, 1917.

———. *Polityka Polska i Odbudowanie Panstwa.* Warsaw: Perzynski, Niklewicz i Ska, 1929.

DIRKSEN, HERBERT VON. *Moscow, Tokyo, London: Twenty Years of German Foreign Policy.* Norman, Okla.: University of Oklahoma Press, 1952.

FILASIEWICZ, STANISLAW. *Le Question Polonaise.* Paris: Section d'Etudes et de Publications Politiques du Comité National Polonais, 1920.

FISCHER, LOUIS. *The Soviets in World Affairs.* New York: J. Cape and H. Smith, 1930.

FISHER, H. H. *America and the New Poland.* New York: The Macmillan Co., 1928.

FRANÇOIS-PONCET, ANDRÉ. *Souvenirs d'une Ambassade à Berlin.* Paris: Flammarion, 1946.

GAFENCU, GRIGORE. *Last Days of Europe, A Diplomatic Journey in 1939.* New Haven, Conn.: Yale University Press, 1948.

GAMELIN, GÉNÉRAL. *Servir.* Vol. I: *Les Armées Françaises de 1940;* Vol. II: *Le Prologue du Drame: 1930–aout 1939.* Paris: Librarie Plon, 1946–47.

GATHORNE-HARDY, G. M. *A Short History of International Affairs, 1920–1939.* London: Oxford University Press, 1950.

GIANNINI, AMEDEO. *La Question de Danzig.* Rome: Instituto per l'Europa Orientale, 1933.

GIBSON, HUGH (ed.). *The Ciano Diaries, 1939–1943.* New York: Doubleday, and Co., 1946.

GRABSKI, STANISLAW. *The Polish-Soviet Frontier.* London: privately printed, 1943.

GRAHAM, MALBONE W. *New Governments of Eastern Europe.* New York: Henry Holt and Co., 1927.

HALECKI, OSCAR. *A History of Poland.* New York: Roy Publishers, 1943.

———. *Borderlands of Western Civilization.* New York: The Ronald Press Co., 1952.

HALIFAX, LORD. *Fullness of Days.* New York: Dodd, Mead and Co., 1957.

HAMMERSTEIN, HANS FREIHERR VON. *Der Waffenstillstand 1918–1919 und Polen.* Berlin: Deutsche Verlagsgesellschaft für Politik und Geschichte, 1928.

HASKINS, CHARLES H., and LORD, ROBERT H. *Some Problems of the Peace Conference.* Cambridge, Mass.: Harvard University Press, 1920.

HENDERSON, SIR NEVILE. *Failure of a Mission, Berlin: 1937–1939.* New York: Putnam's Sons, 1940.

HOUSE, EDWARD M., and SEYMOUR, CHARLES. *What Really Happened at Paris.* New York: Scribner's Sons, 1921.

KOMARNICKI, TITUS. *Rebirth of the Polish Republic, a Study in the Diplomatic History of Europe: 1914–1920.* London: William Heinemann, 1957.

KONOVALOV, S. *Russo-Polish Relations.* Princeton, N.J.: Princeton University Press, 1945.

KOZUSZNIK, DR. B. *The Problem of Cieszyn Silesia.* London: privately printed, 1943.

KUMANIECKI, KAZIMIERZ W. *Odbudowa Panstwowosci Polskiej.* Kraków: J. Czernecki, 1924.

KUTRZEBA, STANISLAW. *Polska Odrodzona 1914–1928.* Warsaw: Gebethner i Wolff, 1935.

KWIATKOWSKI, EUGENJUSZ. *The Economic Progress of Poland.* Warsaw: The Polish Economist, 1928.

LAFFAN, R. G. D. (ed.). *Survey of International Affairs, 1938.* Vols. II and III. London: Oxford University Press, 1951–53.

LAROCHE, JULES. *La Pologne de Pilsudski: Souvenirs d'une Ambassade, 1926–1935.* Paris: Flammarion, 1953.

LLOYD GEORGE, DAVID. *Memoirs of the Peace Conference.* New Haven, Conn.: Yale University Press, 1939.

LUKACS, JOHN A. *The Great Powers and Eastern Europe.* Chicago: Henry Regnery Company, 1953.

LUKASIEWICZ, JULJUSZ. *Z doswiadczen Przeszlosci.* Biblioteka Orla Bialego, n.d.

MACHRAY, ROBERT. *The Poland of Pilsudski.* London: Allen and Unwin, 1936.
———. *The Polish-German Problem.* London: Allen and Unwin, 1941.

MASON, JOHN BROWN. *The Danzig Dilemma.* Stanford, Calif.: Stanford University Press, 1946.

MILLER, DAVID H. *My Diary at the Conference of Paris, with Documents.* 21 vols. New York: privately printed, 1924.

NAMIER, L. B. *Diplomatic Prelude: 1938–1939.* London: Macmillan and Co., 1948.

NOËL, LÉON. *L'Aggression Allemande contre la Pologne.* Paris: Flammarion, 1946.

PHILLIPS, CHARLES. *Paderewski, the Story of a Modern Immortal.* New York: The Macmillan Co., 1933.

PILSUDSKA, ALEXANDRA. *Pilsudski.* New York: Dodd, Mead and Co., 1941.

PILSUDSKI, JÓZEF. *L'Année 1920.* Paris: La Renaissance du Livre, 1929.

POBOG-MALINOWSKI, WLADYSLAW. *Najnowsza Historja Polityczna Polski,* Vol. I. Paris, 1953; Vol. II, Part 1. London: privately printed, 1956.

POLSKIE SILY ZBROJNE W DRUGIEJ WOJNIE SWIATOWEJ. *Kampania Wrzesniowa 1939.* Vol. I. London: Instytut Historyczny im. Gen. Sikorskiego, 1951.

PRZYBYLSKI, ADAM. *La Pologne en Lutte pour ses Frontières, 1918–1920.* Paris: Gebethner and Wolff, 1929.

RACZYNSKI, EDWARD COUNT. *The British-Polish Alliance, Its Origin and Meaning.* London: The Melville Press, 1948.

ROMER, EUGENJUSZ. *Poland: The Land and the State.* New York: Geographical Society, 1917.

ROOS, HANS. *Polen und Europa: Studien zur Polnischen Aussenpolitik.* Tübingen: J. C. B. Mohr, 1957.

ROSE, ADAM CHARLES. *La Politique Polonaise entre les Deux Guerres.* Neuchâtel: Editions de la Baconnière, 1945.

ROSE, WILLIAM J. *The Drama of Upper Silesia.* Brattleboro, Vt.: Stephen Daye Press, 1935.

ROTH, PAUL. *Die Entstehung des Polnischen Staates.* Berlin: O. Liebmann, 1926.

SETON-WATSON, HUGH. *The East European Revolution.* New York: Frederick A. Praeger, 1961.

SEYDA, MARJAN. *Polska na Przelomie Dziejow, Fakty i Dokumenty.* Poznan: Naklad Ksiegarni sw. Wojciecha, 1931.

SFORZA, CARLO. *Diplomatic Europe Since the Treaty of Versailles.* New Haven, Conn.: Institute of Politics Publications, 1928.

SKRZYNSKI, ALEKSANDER. *Poland and Peace.* London: Allen and Unwin, 1923.

SMOGORZEWSKI, CASIMIR. *La Pologne Restaurée.* Paris: Gebethner and Wolff, 1927.

———. *L'Union Sacrée Polonaise.* Paris: A. Costes, 1929.

———. *Poland's Access to the Sea.* London: Allen and Unwin, 1934.

STARZEWSKI, JAN. "Studjum Polski Wspolczesnej: Polska Polityka Zagraniczna w latach 1914–1939," Szkola Nauk Politycznych i Spolecznych. Mimeographed manuscript, London, 1950.

———. "Nowoczesna Historja Polityczna, Rok 1939," Szkola Nauk Politycznych i Spolecznych. Mimeographed manuscript, London, 1954.

STEED, HENRY WICKHAM. *Through Thirty Years: 1892–1922.* Garden City, N.Y.: Doubleday, Page and Co., 1924.

SZEMBEK, JEAN COMTE. *Journal, 1933–1939.* Paris: Librarie Plon, 1952.

TEMPERLEY, H. W. V. *A History of the Peace Conference of Paris.* 6 vols. London: H. Frowde and Hodder and Stoughton, 1920–24.

THE POLISH RESEARCH CENTER. *Poland and the U.S.S.R.: 1921–1941.* Printed as proof, London, 1941.

The von Hassell Diaries: 1938–1944. Garden City, N.Y.: Doubleday and Co., 1947.

TOMMASINI, FRANCESCO. *La Risurrezione della Polonia.* Milano: Fratelli Treves, 1925.

TOYNBEE, ARNOLD, and ASHTON-GWATKIN, FRANK T. (eds.). *Survey of International Affairs, 1939–1946: The World in March, 1939.* London: Oxford University Press, 1952.

—— and VERONICA M. (eds.). *Survey of International Affairs, 1939–1946: The Eve of War, 1939.* London: Oxford University Press, 1958.

WALTERS, FRANK P. *A History of the League of Nations.* Vols. I and II. London: Oxford University Press, 1952.

WHEELER-BENNETT, JOHN. *The Forgotten Peace, March 1918.* New York: Macmillan and Co., 1938.

——. *Munich, Prologue to Tragedy.* New York: Duell, Sloan and Pearce, 1948.

WIELHORSKI, WLADYSLAW. *Polska a Litwa.* London: The Polish Research Centre, 1947.

WITT, KURT. *Die Teschener Frage.* Berlin: Volk und Reich Verlag, 1935.

WOJCIECHOWSKI, ZYGMUNT (ed.). *Poland's Place in Europe.* Poznan: Instytut Zachodni, 1947.

ZOLTOWSKI, ADAM. *Border of Europe.* London: Hollis and Carter, 1950.

Index

PENNSYLVANIA MILITARY COLLEGE
CHESTER, PENNSYLVANIA
LIBRARY

Date Due

APR 4 1968			
DEC 16 '71			
NOV 13 74			
DEC 16			
MAY - 7 2008			

Demco 293-5